Joleta—
Here's to your spiritual health!
— Michelle Collins
11/2017

"create in me

a clean heart, oh God,

and renew a right spirit

within me."

Psalm 51:10
kjv

SPIRIT*CHECK*

Praise for *Spirit Check*

"**Spirit Check** book is a step by step guide for 'checking yourself before you wreck yourself'. It will cause you to take a critical look at yourself and is packed with practical definitions and resources that will promote internal healing and cause you to grow in your mind, body and soul. Michelle was able to state the problems that many have and give wonderful solutions to the ongoing enemy in our lives, which is the struggle between flesh and spirit."
Dr. BJ Strother
M. Div., Ph. Div. Theology

"In my 48 years of ministry, I have reviewed a number of works on the struggles and fleshly pitfalls of humanity. I don't believe I have read a more concise expose' on the identification, and remedy for the challenges each of us deal with in subduing the human, fleshly "spirits" that hinder our onward progress toward spiritual maturity. I highly recommend a thorough reading, and then a methodic application of the principles so proficiently explained in the book, **Spirit Check**."
Bishop Wayne Pense
Heartland America Regional Overseer

"**Spirit Check** book is packed with life-changing information that promotes internal healing. It is a terrific practical resource for anyone that needs to check themselves on a physical, spiritual and emotional level. Michelle was able to find a solution to the ongoing struggle between flesh and spirit, the natural and the super natural , and the internal and the external world."
Kiaundra Jackson
Licensed Marriage and Family Therapist, Mental Health Clinician

SPIRITCHECK

assess your feelings

Unless otherwise noted Scriptures are taken from the New King James Version of the Bible.

Cover design by InZD
Photography by Kathleen Lantos

Printed in the United States of America

ISBN:1974679330
ISBN-13:9781974679331

Contents

Exposing Five: An Introduction   x

And a Spirit Is...   1

Mastering the Emotion. Checking the Spirit   5

How Bold is Bold?   7

The Spirit of Jealousy   9
    The "Only One" Mindset
    Motivational Jealousy
    Signs of Jealousy
    Jealousy Among Friends
    The Cause of Jealousy
    What About Envy?
    Solutions for Jealousy
    What Does the Bible Say About Jealousy?

The Spirit of Intimidation   33
    When Are People Intimidated?
    Signs of Intimidation
    Are You Intimidating?
    What about Manipulation?
    Solutions for Intimidation
    What Does the Bible Say about Intimidation?

The Spirit of Fear   45
    Why we Fear
    The Fear of Success and Failure
    What About Phobias?
    Conquering Fear
    What Does the Bible Say About Fear?

The Spirit of Pride 63

Am I Full of Pride?
False Pride
The Glorification of Victimization
Pride in Action
Overcoming Pride
What About Ego?
What Does the Bible Say About Pride?

The Spirit of Anger 77

How to Identify the Spirit of Anger
Do You Have the Right to Be Angry?
The Cause of Anger
Anger Management
What Does the Bible Say About Anger?

When the Spirits Connect and Collaborate 93

A Word about Strongholds 97

I See You. You See Me. 101

A More Excellent Way 105

The Fruit of the Spirit 117

Now to Deactivate, Finally 121

Acknowledgments
About the Author

"...who can bear a broken spirit..."

Prov. 18:14
kjv

Scripture
Observation
Application
Practice.

Genesis 27: 4

Scripture
Observation
Application
Prayer.

Genesis 2:1-4

Exposing Five: An Introduction

jealousy. intimidation. fear. pride. anger.

There's a brazen agenda coming straight from the enemy's camp to steal, kill and destroy by any means necessary. His target is your emotions, which can seep into your spirit, hoping to make residence there. Once he's set up his means of controlling you, now you become the puppet he uses for massive destruction, first inwardly and then permanently.

Toying with and utilizing your emotions to his advantage is a bullet point on his standard daily schedule. It's a low down, cold and bold move on his part but he's seen success, so he's working his plan. Humans by nature are made up of spirit, soul and body. And if he works it right and in that order, we're done. Literally.

Now enters this book and what I know and what I'll call are the five bold spirits that are not only common emotionally distractions, detractors and destructive but are often living, breathing and growing within us and affecting our lives, negatively. They are **jealousy. intimidation. fear. pride. anger.** The expose' in this book will reveal how these are being used and how to overcome what may be natural, but yet harmful.

It is difficult to admit to yourself much less to anyone else that you may be battling something detrimental until it is first exposed. However, you cannot conquer a thing, unless you first expose that thing. Exposure occurs by some level of self awareness, through the observations of others and especially by the Holy Spirit. Once it is exposed, you can either choose to ignore the call to change your behavior, thinking and attitude or when it is finally revealed, you are going to have to deal with it.

Any attempt to hold on to the reigns of lies will not allow you to live in ultimate freedom. The lie is in not admitting, wanting to cover up and hide your insufficiencies. The message in this book is written on behalf of a Father who desires that we all live in complete alignment with His desire for our lives.

I am by no means insinuating that I am not susceptible to these bold spirits that can creep in and take residence in our heart and destroy our lives. Like everyone else, I can become vulnerable at any given moment. It has been through constant self reflection, self awareness, mindfulness, intentional living, prayer and the Holy Spirit that I have had to not only surrender to self correction, but humbly strive to *"keep my heart with all diligence. For out of it are the issues of life."* Proverbs 4:23

Another disclaimer is that I am not a licensed therapist, counselor or psychologist. As a side note, I did want to obtain a degree in Psychology after my first love for the fashion industry. I have always had a desire to be understood and to understand people's behavior, thoughts and habits. Truth be told, I also wanted to gain a deeper knowledge and understanding of my own.

In part, this book is a personal response to what I have witnessed, experienced or observed that has shaped who I am today. I have encountered, battled against or sometimes even failed to resist these negative and forceful emotions in myself or have seen the negative manifestation of it in others.

These five bold spirits can destroy people, families, ministries and organizations. It is time for mature thinking and living. This is a wakeup call to heal, restore and mend broken hearts, troubled minds and shattered lives.

It is my hope and desire that through this book, a launch of a universal desire will be on each heart to combat the influence and the power of these spirits. I pray we instead adapt a spirit of meekness, commit to taking personal inventory and receive our God given authority, in order to daily overthrow these foul spirits.

Since the five bold spirits are not the problem, but emphatically a symptom of greater issues within oneself, it is important that we take this journey together to reveal some of the underlying issues causing them to manifest.

Make no mistake, you will feel **jealous**, your **anger** will be aroused, **fear** will come upon you, **intimidation** will be present and **pride** will grip you. It is not that you may have subtle experiences, but rather it is being cautious that these spirits don't own you.

The longer that these spirits have you is the more it will control you. I believe it's *on* you then it attempts to live *in* you. It's like a fungus on a nail. You can't just file it down, clip it off or aggressively buffer it. You must get to the root of the spirit, confront it, speak to it that it enters you not again and live in victory over that thing or those things!

Please note that you are limited in your strength and power. And the reality is, you must also be aware that there are certain spirits that will not release their hold over you except by fasting and prayer according to Mark 9:27-29. I'm excited that given time, you will no longer have blurred vision, a skewed perspective and a distorted perception. So, prayers up and fasting in session, unapologetically.

Most people do not realize what is coming from then, what they are emulating or what they are giving off. They are just unaware. It's time to come out of the dark and walk into the light of day.

As you begin to read concerning the spirits, you will be able to not only acknowledge and identify what lies behind even some of your most seemingly unassuming, innocent behavior but also uncover what has forged your attitude and what is controlling your thinking.

While you examine, it is my hope that you will be pricked in your heart to part and sever your tie with the particular stronghold on and over your life. It is preventing you from living your best life, maintaining God ordained relationships and receiving the success you crave and that you were destined to accomplish.

To check your spirit and master your emotions is practicing self love on a daily basis. If it were not important that we take daily stock of our spirit, then the Bible wouldn't admonish us *"Beloved, believe not every spirit, but try the spirits whether they are of God."* I John 4:1. Let's be clear, we are to try our own spirit as well as the spirit of those around us that we interact with or those that interact with our loved ones as well.

How can you try something to see what it is made of, without knowing what it is you are looking for or what it is you must be mindful of? That is the reason this expose' of spirits has been outlined for you. In the chapters that follow, each of the five bold spirits will be dissected.

And as you will notice, there are scripture references and bible lessons. First, I'm a Believer, so my foundation for living is based on the Word of God. When I mentioned that I would be incorporating scripture, someone assured me that making ancient truths relevant and applicable is, well, a good thing.

As I expose the five, let me first share with you what happened to me as I organized my thoughts. The strange thing that occurred is when I began to write about each emotion, it was like I literally felt them come over me, one by one.

The sensation sometimes would last for a few days. It was like God was saying in order for you to passionately share the enemy's bold agenda of these five spirits, I must first make them come alive around you as you write. To sum it up briefly, these are the very personal, various accompanying sensations I experienced for each.

Jealousy | *Annoyance* – Of the five, the bold spirit of jealousy must be the one that is most annoying to the recipient (but dangerous as well). I felt annoyed when I thought of all my personal encounters with those who I was able to identify as jealous of me, past or presently. I had to be very careful not to in turn, get angry (see how quickly one spirit to the next can jump on, within and through you?). Instead, remember that it is a *spirit* of a person and not the person. (More on that later). *Deal with the spirit, Michelle. Deal with the spirit,* is what I told myself and how to do just that is in the forthcoming chapters.

What about the jealousy that flows that flows from us?

Intimidation | *Heaviness* – Wow. There was just such a strong sense of heaviness on my heart as I wrote about the bold spirit of intimidation. It actually made me feel extreme sadness when I realized just how this spirit is being used to nullify God's plan in an individual's life. The bold spirit of intimidation is an oppressor and suppressor. It gets in your mind and will immobilize the impact your footprints have on the earth. You will never be a trailblazer, a change agent or give birth to your dreams if the bold spirit of intimidation rests within you.

Fear | *Fearful* – It's self explanatory that I would feel fear. So almost like intimidation and very much connected to it, the bold spirit of fear will place you in shackles because of your thoughts and mindset. The spirit of fear comes to hamper your potential. In fact, if fear wins, you will never realize just how powerful you already are. Fight. Flight. Freeze. These are elements of fear waiting for you to respond in any one of these ways in your life, daily. The unfortunate thing is we sometimes don't reverse feelings of fear right away. Remember, God has not given us the spirit of fear. So if you feel its presence near, remember what God has given you instead, power, love and a sound mind. This must be declared over your life. Power. Love. A Sound Mind. Say it again, Power. Love. A Sound Mind.

Pride | *Bold* – The bold spirit of pride is indeed very bold but with a facetious spin to it. This wasn't a boldness clothed in Godly confidence. It was more like, *I can do what I want when I want*. I realized that this bold spirit of pride, comes to deceive the person in order to hopefully harm them in the near future. What really stood out for me is the false sense of pride that we all engage in unknowingly. Or as we engage in it, we don't even realize that is what we are doing. This was a big eye opener for me. In fact, uncovering false pride is one of my favorite sections in this book.

Anger | *Anger-* Because the bold spirit of anger likes to hide at first, it is easily covered up. But boy oh boy when it's revealed, it can cause harm and damage in word and deed. While writing about the spirit of anger, I noticed I was raising my voice more because I wanted to ensure that I was being heard. Things that didn't set me off before, I noticed I was getting heated before even attempting to engage in a conversation in love and for clarity. I had to repent many times during the writing about this bold spirit of anger. And as it was the last of the five, I had to be even more mindful of the effect it was having on those around me that I love. I must say here that the bold spirit of anger can be prevalent and the cause of tension, strife and contention and I was not even aware of it. Lord knows that I would've missed this one entirely, had I not begun writing about anger. It creeps in, remains quiet, UNTIL...a button is pushed, a word has offended, old feelings resurface or we experience disappointment. What a powerful spirit. It must be broken.

And there you have the five bold spirits;

jealousy. intimidation. fear. pride. anger.

It is not enough to try and control the outward manifestations of these spirits, it is necessary to repent and move in a different direction all together. Another interesting point to note here is that, the number five is the number of humanity. These Five Bold Spirits are definitely human emotions and feelings by nature. At the same time, in the Bible, the number five symbolizes God's grace. Deeper study of grace suggests that it can be broken into three parts.

There's grace for Unmerited Favor...Grace that is, Virtue from Above...Grace, with access to Divine Assistance. It will require all three functions of grace to combat and stand against these five bold spirits.

Let's keep reading.

And a Spirit Is...

According to the dictionary, a spirit is the *"seat of our emotions and character"*.

It is our inner self, our quiet thoughts and naked mind. Your spirit is the qualities that define your character. It is why you behave like you do, say what you say and think like you think. Your spirit will control your behavior, actions and will affect your attitude. Character, actions and attitude are all indicators of what your spirit consists of.

The spirit is the source that brings our bodies to spiritual life or to spiritual death. This is determined by our choices morally and spiritually. Also, it is with our spirit that we commune with God and in turn His Spirit communes with us.

We are all born with an innate knowledge of good and evil, of right and wrong and an awareness of light and darkness. Once we are "born again" by the Spirit, our spirit desires to move toward that which good and right. That's what our spirit desires. But it is our flesh (nature) that we must bring under subjection.

In the Bible, Paul the Apostle expressed his strategy over temptation and his secret sauce for victorious living as mentioned in I Corinthians 5:13 *"I die daily."* Here he speaks of the battle within and between the Spirit and the flesh that ultimately desires to rule your soul (your mind, intellect and emotion).

The knowledge of just how our spirit functions is essentic
This lays the groundwork to begin the comprehension o
how and when the five bold spirits that will be analyze
in this book may be active or perhaps looming within o
inner person, within our spirit.

Be aware that a spirit can affect you from the OUTSID:
INSIDE or THROUGH OTHERS. You must be watchful an
be alert with each interaction and at all times to protec
your heart, your mind and your soul. Why? Spirits ar
transferable.

Have you ever been feeling down and you get into th
presence of someone who is the exact opposite, full c
life, energy and positivity? Hang around with that perso
for some time and soon their spirit will transfer to you c
you begin to soak up their energy. In the same way, yo
might be in a great mood, but someone enters you
space and they haven't said a word, but their spirit is s
foul, it dampens the entire mood. *LORD DONT LET*
me be a mood Killer
You don't have control of spirits. You only have control c
your flesh. Many times we are controlling our flesh, whic
is good. You should perpetually put your flesh unde
subjection. However, if you haven't dealt with the spirit c
that thing, it will continue to rise up within you an
manifest through your flesh.

And if it's not good, then it's evil. We're dealing with ev
spirits which come to separate you from God, have yo
live in bondage and suppress any good work that ca
come out of you.

For example, you may possess the spirit of envy, but attempt to keep it hidden. At some point, because you have not dealt with the spirit itself, or the underlying issue, your flesh will fail you and expose itself at the opportune time. This is why we must always address the spirit, as you take authority over your flesh as well.

Usually, if you are not "acting like your normal self" then you might exhibit a spirit that is boldly attempting to offset every area of your life. This includes your relationships, business ventures, your goals and even your physical make up.

Wait, there's more.

Mastering the Emotion. Checking the Spirit.

jealousy. intimidation. fear. pride. anger.

The difference between the emotion (or feeling) versus the spirit (which is the seat of our emotions) is that feelings come and go. Feelings aren't always final, neither are they facts you can trust. But it is natural to *feel* these emotions. After all, you're human, aren't you? So freely allow yourself to feel the emotion.

However, it's what you do next that makes the difference between a spirit visiting you and one that you allow to make room on the inside of you. You're angry, but where did you place your anger? Any one of the five bold spirits may come up in you but they should not live within you. CAST DOWN every Imagination

If you allow these spirits to become one with you, it will ultimately be an expression of your mindset and lifestyle. So keep your emotions in check and your spirit clean. Ask yourself, *"Am I living clean or am I riding dirty?"*

This is why you must make it your priority to master your emotions.

We will continue to reveal how to do so in the chapters that follow.

How Bold is Bold?

Ephesians 4:27 says *"Give no place to the devil."*

Be aware that The Five Bold Spirits are seeking a home to live in. And they want to know if through testing and temptation, you will allow them to occupy your mental space. Not temporarily, but permanently.

The enemy wants your mind to be enemy-held territory. He's not asking for permission either. He's got your number, a plan and a strategy of when he will strike. Don't think for a minute that your archenemy doesn't know your tipping points, vulnerable spots and areas of weakness. *Satan has something on his way for you be on guard.*

He's bold in his tactics because that's how you fight and win. By adapting a *I have nothing to lose attitude*, he then uses as tools, some of the same vices that you may possess like fear, intimidation, guilt, unforgiveness, shame... When you buy what he's selling, bingo! He's got you right where he wants you and his move in day has begun immediately. *OH My God!!!*

First the enemy moves in then he builds up. Evicting him at the moving in stage is a lot easier than trying to tear down what he has built up inside of you. This leads us into a conversation on strongholds, which we will address later. But no wonder we are cautioned not to give him a place. In fact, our mental mindset should be *"No Vacancy"*.

You may wonder, how bold is bold? Very bold an
daring. One scripture accurately references the spirit (
jealousy stating *"jealousy is as cruel as the grave."* Son
of Solomon 8:6

And now let's expose these bold spirits one by one...

There have been times in my life when I opened the door for the devil to come in.

We must be able to distinguish between a ambush and when we open the door.

The Spirit of Jealousy

jealousy. *intimidation. fear. pride. anger.*

Jealousy in romantic relationships has been vastly explored. And while that is the number one factor of relationships gone awry, we will examine this bold spirit in totality, not just specifically as it relates to romantic interactions. You may be acquainted on the surface with the bold spirit of jealousy. However, let's take our time to dissect it. This spirit is complex and has several degrees and range.

The dictionary describes jealousy as the following. It says that *jealousy is resentment against a rival, a person enjoying success or an advantage.* Additionally, jealousy is mental uneasiness from suspicion or fear of rivalry or unfaithfulness. Jealousy is an emotional reaction to the scenarios you have played out in your mind that are now affecting your attitude and behavior.

In the words of Serge Benhayon *"Jealousy is nothing more than self fury. It is a personal attack on yourself for not doing what you knew had to be done, which is then vented outward to those who are doing what there is to be done."* Wait, stop right there. So there is a connection between jealousy and "could've", "should've", "would've" and feeling inward pain when you see someone else that "did", "done" and "doing". Ok, we can continue...

Eph. 4:27
And DO NOT
give the devil
foot hold

9

Some of our battles, we opened the Door to.

Ambushed
(2 Chronicles 20)

Also, jealousy is when a person perceives another person to be a threat because of who they are, what they are doing or even what they possess. In another twisted range, for those who are doing, being and having, you may experience a jealousy that says, *I have something that I think you want, that I think you're coming after* (according to Erica Slotter, Professor of psychology at Villanova University).

The Only One Mindset

Here's something we should discuss called "The Only One Mindset". This can be a subconscious belief system that makes you feel a sense of pride (one of the five body spirits) in or because of your unique ability, skill level, material possession, quality or could even extend to natural beauty.

Basically, it is what makes you stand out from the crowd or what comes easy for you but perhaps more difficult for others. Here, you can experience a sense of pride which is not all wrong. Keep reading to understand more once we dissect the spirit of pride. What you need to be careful of is not adapting the belief that you are the only rare breed, superbly blessed to have what you have and do what you do to the point where you look down on others.

If and when you come in contact with or become aware of someone else in your sphere that seemingly or absolutely *also* possesses the manner of things you believe were only unique to you, it's possible to begin viewing them as a rival for the attention that previously only you received, praise or acclaim you want or desire only for yourself.

People can feel threatened by those who they believe want what they already have or feel threatened by those who have what they also have. In essence, you may be the perceived "rival" or become a victim of the "rival" yourself.

However, don't deceive yourself. Some of the most popular individuals at times feel lonely and are insecure human beings. Some highly gifted and talented people are the ones who are also the hardest on themselves. Many successful people are not just climbing the ladder for personal development and to inspire.

It is not uncommon for those people who are the most afraid that they'll lose everything are those whose value and self worth is attached to their accomplishments or material things. If you take away their popularity, status or material possessions, you would be surprised to find that what remains is an unhappy shell, lacking self esteem and self value. Be careful that your ambition is not driven by your insecurity.

Still, according to Dr. Berit Brogaard "people get jealous for no good reason at all". Meaning that, even when there is no obvious sign of a threat, people may experience feelings of jealousy. This has a lot to do with projected jealousy, which is when there is no concrete proof, but in your own thoughts and perceptions, yc rationalize irrational thinking and behavior.

Motivational Jealousy

There is a motivational component to jealousy. Fo example, when you look at your rival, you may b motivated to step up your own game. This in and of itse is not necessarily a terrible thing. Perhaps, you needed t feel the emotion of jealousy to get you going in specific direction that you should've been headed in th first place.

The same goes for seeing a spouse or significant othe who is interacting, connecting or possibly loving o someone else other than you. You may then b motivated to win back or regain their affection by doin things you might have been unmotivated to do before This kind of motivated jealous behavior has actual saved some relationships.

Motivational jealousy arises to essentially motivate you t a specific action or course of actions with hopefully healthy result. Beware, however. Jealousy, in its extrem form can turn you into a person that is unrecognizable See, this bold spirit of jealously will trigger a vast range c emotions that may lead to behavior you could regret.

This is preventable if you become aware and sto jealousy the moment you become aware of its arrival. A a fact, jealousy is the leading cause of spousal homicide

Again, remember the Bible states that *"Jealousy is as cruel as the grave."*

The good news is, when the bold spirit of jealousy presents itself, it is usually an indicator that something needs attention. Jealousy is a sign that someone's needs aren't being met. It's very rare that we will admit to ourselves that we are jealous. Due to feelings of pride (which is another bold spirit), we are afraid (fear is a bold spirit) to become that vulnerable to others, ourselves and even God.

If you seek to identify the source of your jealousy, you can begin the journey of dealing with what is at the root of your emotions. So you may ask yourself, "Are my needs being met?" If not, then decide today to make the necessary changes.

Signs of Jealousy

If I could sum up some of the signs of jealousy, they would be "offering no congratulations, courtesy claps, indifference, undercover insults, severe criticism, imitation and nosiness."

I hope you don't believe that if you ignore the signs, indication or the onset of any of these spirits in yourself or others, that they will miraculously disappear. Wrong! Once you become the recipient, object or target of other people's insecurities and horrible treatment, you will understand very quickly that these spirits are to be handled and dealt with, not and never ever ignored. A I clear?

By nature, my first response is to disassociate myself onc I see the sign(s). I mean, who would willingly sign up to b mistreated or be in an unhealthy relationship c environment? Escaping may work for a time or a seaso however, you will face that spirit again and again. As side note: Did you know that there are some spirits th are assigned to you? Why do you think you often de with the same type of challenges, drama or troubles Pay attention.

And guess what? That spirit may (re)surface in you. So, is in your best interest to learn how to navigate withou losing yourself in the process, whether you are the prey c the perpetrator.

Understand that if you're unhappy when others ar happy, offering them **no congratulations,** doesn't mak their success vanish and neither will the pang of envy your heart. Learn to be okay with other peop succeeding all around you. Tell someone congratulatior no matter how you feel about them personall Especially when you know they've done the work. Yo are not in a position to delegate who deserves wha when nor how. God holds that position perpetually an even at our most undeserving times, He still extenc grace, mercy and favor.

On the other hand, there's a popular quote *"Pay clos attention to those who don't clap when you win".* Ol please note everyone will not applaud you and th certainly does not make individuals automatically jealous of you or highlight those who do not wish you well. Additionally, all those that are clapping may not be necessarily happy for you either.

Perhaps they don't want to feel left out of the celebration. Perhaps they were pressured into clapping also known as "pressure clap". Perhaps they are fawning over your success to take the attention away from their own lack of accomplishments. Perhaps they are living vicariously through you. Perhaps they realize that if they don't clap, you will notice. This is also known as a "courtesy clap". Perhaps they are faking. Perhaps. Perhaps. Perhaps. It's not about those who clap, it's about the content of each heart and who has shown you time and time again, that they care.

Here's a word about **indifference.** You must learn who, what, when and how to share. Know that everyone won't be happy for your great news...and you know who they are. In fact, I know as you read the previous sentence, "everyone won't be happy for you", at least one person came to mind.

If you're going to share, I cannot stress enough how prepared you must be mentally and emotionally for sometimes negative responses you did not solicit. The times you will not be bothered are when you realize that it's not about your news, but it's about how what you shared made them feel. Did you shine light on their unmet need? That is their work to do. It has little to do with you. Carry on. Confidently.

15

Every joke is not a joke and to every joke there is an undertone of truth. Ask any comedian who does standup comedy. Beware if "jokes" railed at you are just undercover **insults**. When a blow needs to be softened, an inserted joke in the form of an insult seems the most likely option. Have you noticed that?

If someone has to make a joke in order to make themselves feel better, or make you feel horrible, it is an indication that they actually have areas in their life where their esteem level is low. Raise your own levels immediately and consistently. They will have to eat their words over and over.

When you're always the topic of bad talk in the form of **severe criticism**, gossiping and putting you down, as if it's open season on our life, then you know for certain there resides a jealous person(s). If they can't or refuse to speak well of you in front of you or behind you, they are most likely partaking in harmful conversations about you.

You must realize that the harm is to them, not you. Again, true friends never criticize to hurt, only to help and it's usually private or one on one. To those that participate in this kind of behavior, if a person's negative ways are affecting you to the degree that you must consistently bring it to the attention of others (usually people who have no power to do anything about it), nothing is changing. It might be more helpful to have an intelligent conversation about your feelings to the individual.

Devaluing one person in the presence of others, only showcases the lack of value you have in your own self.

We all know that whether you're the recipient, a bystander or the instigator of gossip, the negative energy that it breaths can kill your vibes, flow and life. Stop it. I'll insert a favorite quote of mine here "*stop using gossip as a bonding tool*".

Imitation may be one of greatest compliments but not when it comes to the bold spirit of jealousy and feelings of envy. When you have similar tastes and interests as your family or friends, you are bound to display these points of similarities somewhere, somehow. However, copying verbatim someone's move is plagiarism on someone's life.

Cease to trust those who are copy cats. A quote I've used in the past is "*Don't get jealous. Get inspired.*" Unfortunately, some people are not able to execute the latter and indulge in the former at your expense. Keep doing you but keep your eyes open and don't be afraid to switch lanes when you need to.

Nosiness is the pastime and at the core of people who often do not really care. They are more interested in the comparison aspect. The fact that they compare themselves to you is their way of fishing for ways to ensure you haven't surpassed them in life, even a little.

When you truly care about someone or a situation, you naturally take the steps needed to show them. Eventually, everyone will know you care or don't care by the actions you take or do not take. When they ask just for knowledge or are being overly curious for updates,

that may very well be a sign of them making certain the
you are not doing better than them.

Them, *"Did you find a job?"*

You, *"No, still looking."*

Them, *"Mmmm, Ok."* Possibly thinking, *"So no steac
income which means she/he can't fund their dreams.*

There are numerous more signs of the bold spirit o
jealousy including the ones who always seek to upstag
you, or are interested in leveling the playing field an
even downgrading your hard earned accomplishment
I believe your eyes are wide open even more now. Yo
are more familiar with the bold spirit of jealousy than eve
before.

Jealousy among Friends

It has been documented by psychologists that *we lov
our friends, but we love meeting our own needs more
We usually only feel happy for someone else, when w
already feel happy for our own selves.* I'm sure yo
recognize this statement as true already. How importar
is it then, to keep growing into who we can become
This will help to ensure we are not consistently givin
others the side eye as God allows expansion to com
into their lives.

Jealousy among friends can be disheartening. Man
people are unhappy in their world.

So they are constantly escaping into the world of others (being curious, nosy). They are looking for any justification that will allow them to feel better in their world again. Some people seem to make this their 9-5 job and personal assignment.

If you find yourself desiring what is present in your friend's life, it is only an obvious indication of the absence of that very thing in your own life. It is unfair to your friend for you to go down a path of jealousy, envy, resentment and bitterness. You shouldn't make people feel bad for what they have or who they innately are, simply because you desire those things yourself.

A healthier approach is to seek to fill in the emotional gaps of what's missing in your own life. Filling in emotional gaps are imperative here but our behavior and attitude are usually materialistic. We tend to want to fill emotional gaps with material goods.

An example is, your friend just bought a new car, so shortly thereafter; you buy a new car as well. Perhaps your friend has been saving up for years to buy the car but you want to deplete your bank account in order to numb that jealous feeling. The lesson here would be to focus on filling in the emotion that's driving you to numb what apparently needs your attention. Take the time to do that, before you spiral out of control.

The Cause of Jealousy

So here are some causes of the bold spirit of jealous One root of jealousy is **fear** (another bold spirit). So it imperative that you take some time to unpack what it that you are afraid of. What is it that you are really fearf of? Once you identify the source, then you can begin t deal and confront it, head on.

The usual suspect for feelings of jealousy, are tied to lo self esteem. This means, that you have a sense of beli that has produced a false mental image. In essence, yc believe that "you are not good enough", even as you t to convince yourself and others, that you are. Dee right?

Self Sabotage is also a work of jealousy. We can feel s overwhelmed by our success or favor, that we allo ourselves to find ways to destroy it. This goes back to se worth and whether or not we feel we deserve what w have. If you are an insecure person, you probab dabble in self sabotage from time to time.

By continuing to engage in self sabotage, you will driv away success, love and great experiences that ar available to you. And the very thing you are afraid c losing, will eventually slip away because of your though and behavior.

So then you can become jealous of what you see others, even though it resides in you as well. Th difference is someone else has triumphed over fear an manage to cripple the works of self sabotage but whe

20

you look within your own self, you self loath because you recognize, you may not have done the same. Investing thoughts in what you fear or what you're insecure about, will only lead to more fear and more insecurity. Stop the thoughts in their track.

Begin to appreciate the value in others, especially if what you see in them, you also recognize within yourself. That is probably one of the best ways to connect with others is through your similarities. Which is interesting that even though similar, (both of you are working your way to the top, both of you enjoy some of the same experiences, both of you are on the stage receiving an award, both of your pictures are on the same event flyer, both of you can collaborate for success at any time) it is that same all too similarity that people sometimes allow unnecessary separation and tension, also known as discord, to occur.

Even though you're similar, your fingerprint, foot print and blue print is very different. You don't have to run from what's familiar because you see it as a threat. Watch closely, you may learn something new. Better yet, find something to add to your own repertoire. So the next time you see something similar in someone else that you know lies within you as well, don't quickly run away or see them as an immediate threat. I challenge you instead, to view it with a fresh set of eyes of appreciation.

What about Envy?

Proverbs 27: 4 "Wrath is cruel and anger is outrageou but who is able to stand before envy?"

I would do this book a disservice if I didn't address th popular first cousin of jealousy. We've already define the bold spirit of jealousy, but underlining and sometime supporting jealousy is a creature called **Envy**. Whi jealousy is seeing others as a threat to what you have possess, envy is wanting or desiring what someor already has.

I read an article that referenced a study published in th Journal Science which showed that when we feel env it activates a region of the brain involved in processin physical pain. The spectrum of envy can range in th following ways, material possessions, physic attractiveness, money, fertility, relationship status, weigh professional success and so on. Envy manifests when person comes up or believes they have come up sho usually based on comparison or competition.

What is needful to understand is that waiting at the do of envy are two friends, depression and anxiety. Yo must seek fulfillment and find ways to have your person needs met. This will block feelings of envy from comin into your spirit.

Let us also be clear, that having what you desire someone else, is not a guarantee that you will have th same experience as you believe they have (had Remember the example of buying a new car ju because your friend bought one? Know that your experience with the same car will be different. You could face car troubles you are not equipped to handle, while their car seems to run seamlessly. That's life. There are no guarantees to happiness. The only solution is found within when you do the inner work to achieving your own greatness and making your own mark in this big, wonderful world we live in.

A person that is envious is guided by their own vicious ego. The ego is so enlarged that they will never admit that they are envious in the first place because that would mean that they are inferior to the subject of their envy. Their sole mission is to see the person that they are envious of unhappy, sad or experience something negative. They are happy when negativity occurs or they are a product of the cause. Either way, stay away from, build borders around and create boundaries for people who are envious.

Did you know that envy might not show up in relationships until later? For example, on the surface level, you may be deceived that a person is drawn to you solely for who you are. Only to realize that their attraction to you is based on what they see you already have and what they desire for their own selves.

Have you ever had someone come close, get to know you, may even offer what seems like support but eventually they vanish? Not disappear in the sense that you don't see them anymore. But more so, they're doing

things quite similarly to how you've done it but now fro
a far distance.

It will make even more sense when you realize that it
those who you have brought close that are the on
mimicking or despising your every move. Yo
relationship with them will soon change from attractic
to hostility on either your part or theirs. Simply becaus
tension will arise whether by them trying to achieve wh
you have or when you finally realize that you have
snake in the grass as a "friend", or a "supporter".

So keep a watchful eye of even your inner circle. B
aware of excessive praises, pats on the back, rubs on th
shoulder and high fives. There are always exception
However, these common indicators are usua
preparation for the ultimate blow coming down th
pipe. Jesus had twelve disciples and one of the
betrayed Him. Let that sink in.

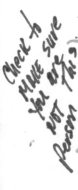

Solutions for Jealousy

Are you ready to get on a path to eradicate the bo
spirit of jealousy? Now that you're aware, you must beg
to change your false belief system. You have to spea
believe and act the very opposite of whatever lies yo
have been telling yourself, or allowed yourself to believe

This is going to take some time of you being intention
about it. Because in order to change the mind to birth
new thought pattern, it will only come from repeated

doing what is necessary for true mental transformation. So here are a few reminders.

Remember, one person's success does not automatically equal your failure.

Remain grateful. When you count your blessings, it won't be difficult to subtract the need to focus on what you don't have. Grateful people exude joy, peace and contentment.

Investing in quality time with yourself will help to boost your confidence as opposed to secretly wishing you had someone else's life.

If you're constantly in comparison mode, how can you truly enjoy what you already have? That must be the reason Theodore Roosevelt said "*Comparison is the thief of joy.*" You must remember that others will always have what we don't have or be privy to various experiences that we won't. And that's okay. You're only missing 100% of the shots that you don't take.

Build your self esteem by living your potential and becoming better at what and who you already are. Self esteem comes from your ideal self in comparison to your sense of self. If your hope is to be more of who and what you are, then your self esteem is high. If you are constantly comparing your sense of self to your ideal self and not measuring up, you might feel low, depressed and even angry. Therefore, since you've adopted the believe system that you cannot attain who you're trying to become by yourself, you will seek the closest person to you to project your envy on.

Go to Therapy.

Get a course on Self Esteem.

Take the time to focus on your own growth and personal development.

Keep yourself busy.

Make better choices. Let your life reflect the opportunities you chose to take advantage of, not the ones you regret. Better choices will undoubtedly create a sense of fulfillment. Know that each moment has created an opportunity for you to make new choices at any time. What can you choose differently today?

What Does the Bible Say about Jealousy?

There are numerous recordings in the Bible of the Bold Spirit of Jealousy and so many great lessons to learn from each scenario with characters that were flawed, yet still chosen by God.

1. *"When Joseph's brothers saw that their father loved him more than all of them, they hated him and could not speak peaceably to him."* Gen 27:4

   a. Is it Joseph's fault that his father loved him more? Was it that his father loved him more or that his father loved him differently? When we see the story unfold, Joseph was indeed chosen. In the end, God used Joseph to deliver his own family out of a drought.

b. Sometimes we hate people for their ability to connect with others. It does not take away from your own gifting and abilities. There is a purpose and a design as to why God made you the way you are and why He made others the way He made them. Try not to be overly sensitive. It usually makes sense later.

c. Not speaking to Joseph because he was favored is one of the greatest acts of immaturity. And they were his older brothers! He was the youngest, the least experienced, the one that would have to wait his turn. Yet they hated him for who he was, even though his birth order, personality and charisma were beyond his control. Beware of people who hate you just for being you. Don't let that hinder you. You are valuable, needed and there is a plan for you.

and others who hate others because of them

2. *"And they gathered themselves together against Moses and against Aaron, and said unto them, Ye take too much upon you, seeing all the congregation are holy, everyone of them, and the Lord is among them: wherefore then lift ye up yourselves above the congregation of the Lord?"* Numbers 16:3

a. Here's a classic case of sabotage of leadership. Moses was appointed by God. Literally. He was

timid and was not the best speaker. Yet Gc
chose Him to lead God's people out of th
bondage of Egypt into the promised land
Canaan. Moses did as God commanded. No
here Moses is *continuing* as God's chose
leader and as if on cue, a few rise up again
him and begin to question his authority to c
what it is he had been doing all along
leading! He might not have been perfect, b
he was faithful.

b. It's interesting here to note that when othe
have a problem with your position, wheth
appointed or anointed, they can't keep th
jealousy or envy to themselves. They always fir
others to join in with them, to support the
efforts of sabotage. They create a group to s
ambush for a takeover or a takedown.

c. If you find that you have to gather people f
your negative mission, it will eventually turn c
you. Leave others alone. Maybe they weren
thinking along the same lines that you wer
thinking. Even if they were thinking it, mayb
they were not prepared to act out on the
thoughts. Now here you come with you
agenda to stir discord. Can we not wo
together and support each other without th
negativity?

3. *"And Saul was very wroth, and the sayin
displeased him. And he said, They have ascribe
unto David ten thousands and to me they hav*

28

ascribed but thousand: and what can he have more but the Kingdom? And Saul eyed David from that day and forward." I Samuel 18:9

a. Saul. Saul. Saul. You might not have liked what the people said. It hurt your feelings. You were offended. We understand. Every now and then our ego gets bruised. But Saul, the *people* said it. David didn't say a word. David fought the battle and won the battle by killing Goliath. Remember that? Remember how David stepped up to the plate when no one else would? He defeated the enemy. So why do you have a problem with David? He helped you and the kingdom gain the victory! He came just in the nick of time. He's a 17 year old shepherd boy. You're the King! What do you and David have in common? Nothing! Yet, you laser focused on David because other people sang his praises.

b. Keep a watchful eye on the room when you're receiving accolades, awards, compliments, a promotion or gifts. The Bible wouldn't declare in Psalm 23:5 *"You prepare a table before me in the presence of mine enemies"* if there weren't enemies to prepare a table in front of. I cannot tell you the amount of times that I have been speaking in front of a crowd and when I look out, I see individuals sloughed in their seat, seemingly to avoid making eye contact with me. I know you're there. I know where you're sitting. You're sitting in the same spot you were

prior to me walking on stage. You can't hic
from me. Also, be mindful of those who w
leave the room. It's like suddenly a bathroo
break becomes most urgent, hosting their ow
personal workshop in corners or down the hc
and even outside. Some of these are harmle
but some are blatant jealousy, env
resentment and bitterness. Has this ev
happened to you?

c. When I was growing up and even still in th
present, it made me so uncomfortable wher
would receive compliments. This was for tw
reasons. I was super self-conscious therefore
didn't want unnecessary attention on m
People would say "*Oh she loves the attention*
And I would try to convince the room "*No,
really don't*" because of the very thing that wc
happening. All were eyes on me (Ughh!) ar
all eyes on me didn't necessarily mean all ey
are *for* me. Somewhere I instinctively knew the
negative spirits were looming like clouds waitin
to rain on what was a parade that I didn
initiate. You must know that compliments fro
one will stir resentment in others.

4. "*And the next Sabbath day came almost th
whole city together to hear the Word of God. B*
when the Jews saw the multitudes, they were fille
with envy, and spake against those things whic
were spoken by Paul, contradicting an
blaspheming" Acts 13:44-45.

a. People will become jealous and envious of your influence. Let's be clear that this was again nothing you initiated. You're working your gift, walking in obedience and tapping into who God has called you to be. It's not you. It's the impact of your work that will have people questioning their own ability and obedience to show up in their own life. The next step is for people to begin to speak negatively about you and try to distract from your good work with their bad behavior. Don't get discouraged. Keep working. They have their reward coming and you have yours.

The Spirit of Intimidation

*jealousy. **intimidation**. fear. pride. anger.*

The definition of intimidation is to make timid or fearful: especially to compel or deter by or as if by threats. People who intimidate are inducing fear or a sense of inferiority into another. It is the reduction to a state where the spirit is broken or all courage is lost. Intimidation can be projected consciously and unconsciously. Often, bullies intimidate through threats, insults or aggressive behavior.

We often teach our children not to fear bullies but to learn to stand up for themselves. Most important is we secretly hope that our own children do not participate in bully-like behavior. There are campaigns, workshops, events, apparel and even infomercials that speak against bullies and the need for peace and harmony in schools and on campuses. Yet, there is one demographic that will be brought to the forefront in this book and that is, adults who are bullies and adults that intimidate.

Did you not know that adults can also project and display bully-like behavior? Usually when you intimidate another person, you are foremost placing fear of bodily injury. However, not all cases of intimidation result in physical threat or bodily harm. For example, this bold spirit of intimidation can include a look of dislike, discontent or anger, verbal abuse, purposeful

embarrassment, underhanded tactics. All these co
cause emotional injury to the person being intimidated.

(Out of all the bold spirits, the spirit of intimidation make
me feel very gloomy and disappointed becaus
although it is by law a criminal offense, the emotion
scars can be damaging and the symptoms
intimidation can deter individuals from fulfilling their Goc
given purpose at the hands of someone who usua
knows better.)

Intimidation is powerful because it needs focuse
intention to be successful. The intimidator must know th
vulnerabilities of their prospect, including the victim
lack of assertiveness. They may conceal their behavic
set limitless ambush, they are ready to be ruthless whe
needed and become physical if necessary. Intimidato
craft their actions so that who they intimidate will b
submissive to their grander scheme in place.

Since the intimidator's goal is to bring the individu
under subjection, they will condition their victims to avoi
upsetting, confronting or contradicting the manipulatc
How many times have you wanted to speak up again
wrongdoing towards you or others? You may hav
thought the repercussions if you confront, far outweighe
the need for exposure or justice.

When are People Intimidated?

You might have seen the memes depicting intimidatio
on social media. Usually there is an image of a large
person or animal showing dominance over a much lesse
34

frame of a person or animal. That is the picture we have in our head when we think of intimidation. We think of a cat intimidated by a lion or a less experienced young person intimidated by a more mature and successful adult. While both of those scenarios are common, intimidation and the emotion of feeling threatened by someone is not limited to greater than versus less than.

It is very possible for the script to be flipped. You can be intimidated by your subordinate. And if you are the subordinate, this might come as a surprise to you. It might have little or a lot to do with your age, physical attributes, abilities, skill level and even your demeanor of confidence. People will become intimidated because you are the object of what they wish they possibly had and may feel they will never attain to.

Did you know always doing a good job can cause people to be intimidated by you? They may glare or poke holes in what everyone else is showing praise for. If you have strong work ethic, it might be deemed as you are trying to prove just how much less everyone else is at accomplishing their task. Your brilliance might be shining so brightly that you unknowingly have put out the flame in those who previously had the spotlight. This frequently occurs when you are the new person in a group, a class, at work or in any social setting. Or it's just your season of blessings and prosperity.

Signs of Intimidation

The bold spirit of intimidation can arise over time but al:
very quickly. Watch for sudden changes in the reactic
of those who were once singing your praises and no
seemingly find fault with everything you do, or agree wi
those who are finding fault against you. Those that see
to intimidate will now set out to undermine, criticize ar
poke holes. It is their way of hoping to throw you off ar
a part of their master plan to cause you to give up.

Those that posses the spirit of intimidation, will participat
in blocking your next and every move. It might be tim
for a promotion, but their hope is that by all the ho
poking and criticism that you've experienced at the
hand, it will cause you not to speak up about it becaus
of the fear factor. They will never offer your name up fe
recommendation. If you happen to come up
discussion, they will present every reason why you shou
be overlooked or simply not speak up on your behc
when it is in their power to do so.

Intimidators seek to block as well when they have acce
in certain spaces, places or with people you do not. The
are promotion blockers, blessing hecklers and wedge
between the possibilities of your advancement. They w
even stand as an "in between" even though it's no
necessary.

They will volunteer to be your voice, a messenger or th
delivery person when there clearly is no need. It is the
way of ensuring you do not surpass them on the
level. They know, that if given the opportunity, th

36

moment, space and time, you would impress the higher ups and receive a promotion that far outweighs their previous efforts.

You know the meager assignment you've been given? It's not that it's beneath you or you are too prideful to perform it. But those that carry the bold spirit of intimidation love to ensure that their victims are doing the lowest of impact and the lowest of visibility kind of work. They might even assign or recommend you for something they know you cannot handle, just to see you fall flat on your face.

This is to keep you at the certain level they want you, lest you shine for others who they hold in high regard, see you in your rightful position. They will leave you out of group texts, meetings and gatherings you were suppose to participate in. Keep your head up. You've done nothing wrong. In due season, everyone will reap what they sow.

Intimidators really wish in their heart of heart that you would just disappear. Try not to be surprised when they stop offering support, showing up for dates that are important to you, and relatively withdraw from you. It may cause you to feel lonely. You will feel like you are on your own and that's because you probably are.

The less they see you, the less of a threat you propose. The more they see you, is the more they will try to bring you down to size. Let that negative energy and foul spirit return to where it came from and do not entertain it for one second. Keep up your good work and let the spirit intimidation devour itself.

Are You Intimidating?

Have you ever been told that you are intimidating? have. And although at any given time, what is perceive by others is their reality, I beg to differ. People cc mistake strong personalities as an act of intimidation. W have all experienced at one time or another, ho individuals with a strong personality can overpower meeting, a room, a space and certainly a conversation don't necessarily believe that's me (one wh overpowers). It could be that my persona could k intimidating not necessarily my position or the intent my heart. But I digress.

There is a lot to consider in these scenarios as we kno quite well that people show up with personal agend from time to time. However, to be intimidating, you mu consistently showcase your strong arm with all those wh come in contact with you. It's your lifestyle. It's abo consistency in actions, not perception of thoughts.

We are the total of our experiences and while not all us have used the ingredients to purposefully cause harn most people that consistently come off as too strong are aggressive, do so because they "feel" they need t Somewhere and in some part of their life they learne that wearing a mask is not comfortable anymore an pretense is exhausting and unnecessary. This will b mistaken for intimidation to those who love drama, make excuses and aren't solution oriented.

Usually people who are intimidating have invested time in educating themselves and personal development which has afforded them the ability to engage in conversations that matter, creating opportunities, having survival instincts and are the keepers of their word. They see all opposites as daunting, so it is not surprising that their circle is relatively small.

People who seem intimidating are often misunderstood. Usually, and I express this with a grain of salt, they are people who once you get to know them, they aren't so bad after all. But that's just it. You will need to take the time necessary to get to know them, if they let you in. They realize everyone won't do that, so they keep it moving.

I mean, how many of us really have the time to ensure we are understood by the masses? There is no need to validate your authenticity. Those that love you, will get it. Those that don't, you probably don't need them in your circle anyway.

Recognize that sometimes you can gleam from people that seem intimidating, for your own personal growth. However, they tend to attract jealousy and envy as well, especially from those who are unwilling to do the inner work or recognize the areas of improvement needed in their own lives. I am not suggesting that we all become intimidating people. But it does behoove us to adapt qualities of growth for personal success patterns.

Solutions for Intimidation

Here are additional action steps in fighting against th bold spirit of Intimidation that is strong armed agair you.

This spirit comes to suppress you and prevent you fro becoming all that God designed for you to becom Get rid of your stinking thinking. You need a mind sh and a reset in your thoughts. When God created you, F had a purpose and a plan for your life. One of n favorite quotes is *"God had a plan long before anyor had an opinion."* Let it resonate that God does not nee anyone's help in accomplishing what He has in mind fu you.

You place people in the wrong position when you plac them in positions that are before God and you deper on their approval before you can make any move your life. Keep God at the head, in front and on tc where He belongs. It is He whose hands people's hec rests in.

That means that God is in control and no one can revok His authority in the earth and over your life. Not eve those whose use strategy to intimidate can intimidat God out of doing what He wants for you. If God is nc bothered, you shouldn't be either. My quote? *"B unbothered like God."*

You might make it a challenge to drop your fear an walk up to those who you feel have an air c intimidation. Be yourself. Try to prove nothing. Start a interesting conversation. Let them know that you are in the room as well and you appreciate the good qualities of those who make the effort that is admirably in the plight of success. A favorite quote of mine is *"Don't you dare get a seat at the table and then be intimidated by who's already there. Whether by hard work or God's favor, you deserve to be where you are just as much as the next person."*

What about Manipulation?

If envy is the first cousin of jealousy, then manipulation is the twin sister of intimidation. Both are a means to not just control, but have domination over an individual. Fear is used in intimidation, and deceit is common in manipulation. However, manipulation requires an acute skill level to accomplish total control.

Manipulation can occur from child to parent, spouse to spouse, colleague to colleagues and the list can go on. The thread is that a manipulator utilizes guilt and shame as a means to control how the individual responds to excessive requests by the manipulator.

This is why it is important to rid yourself of all inward shaming and release what has been done and what is out of your control. Are you familiar with the Prayer of Serenity? *"God grant us the serenity to accept the things we cannot change, the courage to change the things we can and the wisdom to know the difference."*

No one can hold anything over you, if you are n
holding on to it first. Manipulators have done du
diligence in studying you and what you may be feelir
guilty or shameful about. But somehow they feel neith
guilt nor shame about their own manipulative ways.

Knowing your vulnerabilities will provide a protectiv
barrier against those who look for spaces whe
vulnerability lies.

Do you have the disease to please?

Do you lack assertiveness?

Are you self doubting?

Low in self confidence?

As much as the enemy uses people to advance h
agenda, you should be doing double duty to thwart h
plan.

Keep reading. But first...

What Does the Bible Say about Intimidation?

Very often the scenarios of intimidation mentioned in th
Bible have to do with armies that were more equippe(
larger in size or more skilled at winning battles. There ar
other mentions of leaders, disciples and apostles wh
were carrying out the work of the Lord, but someho
needed a boost in confidence to face their enemy (
intimidators.

And in every opportunity, the Bible has declared everything from encouragement to trust in God, being courageous, standing firm in Godfidence, doing the work, not giving in and be strong. Here are scriptures that encourage and shed light on intimidation.

"Study to show thyself approved..." is what 2 Timothy 2:15 encourages us to do.

"Masters do the same to them, and stop threatening them knowing that he who is both their Master and yours is in heaven and that there is no partiality with him". Eph 6:9

"Be strong and courageous. Do not fear or be in dread of them, for it is the Lord your God who goes with you. He will not leave you or forsake you." Deut 31:6

"What then shall we say to these things? If God is for us, who can be against us?" Rom 8:31

"Do not fear those who kill the body but cannot kill the soul. Rather fear him who can destroy both soul and body in hell." Matt 10:28

"So Moab was in great fear because of the people, for they were numerous..." Numbers 22: *Numbers 14*

Here's a quick nugget. Don't tell God about your problems. Tell your problems about God. He likes to manifest Himself strong and mighty with few, not the majority. Large numbers, big sizes, the swarm of the crowd are all eligible for Him to showcase His mighty acts in and through you.

"He was hired for this reason that I might becom frightened and act accordingly and sin, so that the might have an evil report in order that they cou reproach me." Nehemiah 6:1

Don't doubt whether or not certain people have bee assigned for a particular season of your life. Ar sometimes they're positioned as a set up for your trc that leads to your fall. Who has the devil assigned late to you? Food for thought. *wow!!!*

The Spirit of Fear

*jealousy. intimidation. **fear.** pride. anger.*

The dictionary says that Fear is an unpleasant emotion caused by the threat of danger, pain or harm. Fear is released when you perceive the threat of danger is near. It can cause a person to flee, hide or freeze up in response to present fear or in anticipation of a future threat.

According to Dr. Karl Albrecht, those who make you feel fearful will also make you angry. For example if you are fearful of an oppressor, competitor or opponent, you will become angry at them. Your anger is positioned as a way to deal with the fear you feel.

There are moments when you numb your fear in order to avoid or to escape. This would include declining to participate in certain activities that you perceive will embarrass you or you perceive you are inadequate to complete. This would also include not wanting to take a certain medication because you fear the side effects, turning down an invitation to a party because you feel uncomfortable in a group setting, lack of commitment to your partner because of the fear of future infidelity. And so on.

The downside here is that there are definite destiny moments and purpose filled assignments that are predestined by God on your behalf. My fear is that you are letting fear get the best of you by living in suppressed, oppressed and eventually depressed stat simply because you have not or will not step out of fe and walk in liberty. "_Therefore if the Son makes you fre you shall be free indeed._"John 8:36

God has given us many blessings and fear is not one them. What He has designed for you, come to make yc greater and many times does take you out of o comfort zone. And He does this on purpose.

How will you ever grow and experience new depths ar higher heights in Him if you stay stuck in what's familia Your potential becomes stagnant, your creativity suppressed and you miss an opportunity to rise to th occasion when you fall in love with your comfort zone.

Comfort zone according to one theory is in reference the temperature zone (67 to 78 degrees) where we ar most comfortable and feel neither hot nor cold. In th book of Revelations 3:15 -16 God says "_I wish you wer either cold or hot. So then because you are lukewarn and neither cold nor hot, I will vomit you out of m mouth._" What a thought that remaining "comfortable upsets God's stomach. It means you are not living up t the potential He placed inside of you. And that make Him sick. Ouch.

Many are living lukewarm temperature lives and i relationships and God is not digesting it. He' much rather you take a stand. Stand in the heat c sit and freeze in the cold. I dare say that thos that are lukewarm are sitting down comfortably, possibly in fear.

Exercising fear is a natural response to being in the presence of those who are superior than you or those who you perceive are more powerful than you. The enemy of your soul has the audacity to flex his God given, God allowed power on a consistent basis.

But you must remind yourself that he is already defeated and is on borrowed time. Don't let him trick, lie or deceive you into thinking that the same power that raised Jesus up from the dead, does not lie within you. It does. Exercise your authority and speak to the bold spirit of fear and it will have to bow.

The spirit of fear will also reside in those who know that they have done wrong. They fear that at any moment the wrong that they have done will eventually catch up to them. You may as well, live in fear because of sin in your own life that remains as a constant reminder that you are contradicting the word of God.

God has not condemned you. Instead, he has created opportunities for you to get back in alignment. It is up to you to make haste that His perfect will, not His permissive will, will be made manifest, not out of fear but out of necessity.

Why We Fear

According to psychologists, fear is a learned behavior and could be based on a traumatic experience. This trauma that is replayed in the head could be something experienced personally or by observation.

Fear can be passed on from persons, generations ar even cultures. In other words, if your mother was fearf of dogs, then you could develop that same fear as we It really takes an intentional mindset to break this bo spirit in order that it not produce a stronghold in your life

Whenever we give in to negative thinking, we allow fe to seep in and we will become irrational. Negativ thinking includes worry, anxiety or dread. Again, we w experience the product of stinking thinking.

It had been probably 15 years that I went to c amusement park. And in the past, if I did you would n find me riding on any roller coaster. On a recent fami trip to a theme park with my family, I was prepare mentally to sit out any ride that gave me the impressic that it was fast and furious.

You see, the last time many years ago I was tempted go on a roller coaster, I suddenly changed my mind. didn't understand why at the time but in retrospect, was probably my intuition because I later found out I wc pregnant. So all these years, I carried the fear of the roll coaster experience and I was proud of my fear.

So on this recent family trip, I joined the line with m crew. I didn't back out, even though I was afraid c what the experience might entail. And you know what? did it! In fact, I went on rides that you wouldn't hav caught me on a year prior. You want to know somethin else? It wasn't that terrible. Ok, granted even thoug I hunched over clinging on to whoever was sitting next t me for dear life, I made it through. I survived. And in spite of apprehension, an attachment to a negative memory and fear, you can as well.

Not knowing what the future lies, can cause the spirit of fear to set in. The future could be after death, the next 20 years or even tomorrow. It is here that I must reference the scripture which says *"Let not your heart be troubled..."* St. John 14:1. See if the enemy can get you to focus and be fearful or worried about the unknown, then He has caused you to take your eyes off of God, who is your present help now. Learn to release every unknown thing to the all knowing God, especially our future by placing it in His hands.

The Fear of Success and Failure

Let's talk about the twins "Success and Failure". The fear of success and failure which tends to be based on the ego, must be discussed. Do you recall the story of Jonah in the Bible? God had given him instructions to go preach to the people of Nineveh and he was fearful of what the people would say or do to him.

There are many of you who could've possibly been further ahead in your career, relationship, business and your life if you weren't so caught up and tangled up in OPP also known as Other People's Opinions. You must remember an opinion is not a fact.

To be true or false it must be a fact, not an opinion. An opinion is how a person feels and an opinion cannot

cannot be proven. You will never be able to plea
everyone whether by opinion or facts for that matter.

Usually your fear of success or failure is also based
doubting yourself, your capabilities or even your worth.
is in these times that recalling who you are in Christ ar
seeing yourself the way He sees you, will eliminate the:
paralyzing thought patterns. Once you move past the
you must then move forward to accomplish the task
hand that you are most fearful of. If you don't you w
continually be plagued by fear, because fear will n
go until confrontation challenges it. Take your pow
back and fear will have to find a new home.

Here is what may be behind your fear of success. I'
exposing them one by one. You might be exhibiting fe
for one of the following reasons:

You are afraid that others will become jealous of you.

You are afraid you might gain more enemies.

You are afraid it (success) will be taken from you.

You are apprehensive that you might experience failure

You are afraid that you will lose friends.

You are afraid you will attract the wrong kind of friends.

You are afraid that you will be lonely.

You are afraid of appearing unspiritual.

You are afraid of being called too spiritual.

You are afraid to stand out.

You are afraid of rejection.

You are afraid of the attention.

Here's what you now need to realize. Success is here not to make you feel powerless. Success makes you empowered to overcome whatever myths fear places in front of you. But you must take the steps to success in order to be relieved of fear. You are more powerful than you think. You have always been powerful.

Fearing success is normal because it means you are about to enter unchartered territory. Who wouldn't feel the least bit anxious or nervous wondering if they have what it takes to win the challenge? Listen, you've made it this far. That is a good indication that you possess what's needed to continue on your journey. Don't stop now. Keep going. You should be excited!

I remember a time in my life that I was feeling apprehension about what I'll call "the difference". This is the gap between who you were and what you're becoming. You can become fearful to jump and close the gap for all of the above reasons and more. However, you're doing yourself a disservice if you don't realize that everything you are (becoming) has always been in you. It's not a new you. You are walking into an evolved version of yourself.

So don't let others convince you with a negative connotation that you have changed. And certainly don't beat yourself up because you don't want to seem

different. This new version of yourself? It's always bee
inside of you. Now embrace yourself in totality. Dor
think of it as a difference or subtraction from you b
instead view it as an addition or multiplication to yo
See, most of your inner victories lies within gaining a ne
perspective on how you view what could be deemed
failure.

I was in my late twenties when I was first introduced
the following quote by Marianne Wiliamson. And still
this day, it remains one of my favorites. Sometimes I wish
had come across it earlier in my life. I'm sure it would'
guided many of my prior decisions.

*"Our deepest fear is not that we are inadequate. O
deepest fear is that we are powerful beyond measure.
is our light, no our darkness that most frightens us. We a
ourselves, Who am I to be brilliant, gorgeous, talente
fabulous? Actually, who are you not to be? You are
child of God. Your playing small does not serve th
world. There is nothing enlightened about shrinking s
that other people won't feel insecure around you. W
are all meant to shine, as children do. We were born
make manifest the glory of God that is within us. It's n
just in some of us; it's in everyone. **And as we let our ow
light shine, we unconsciously give other peopl
permission to do the same.** As we are liberated from o
own fear, our presence automatically liberates others.*"

This. Changed. My. Entire. Perspective. I had no idea th
I had been standing in my own way because of the fea
that resided within me. Do you mean that when I'r

walking in fear I'm working against God's plan and not in sync with His will for my life? I was allowing the opinions of others to be magnified in my mind and blaming them as the source behind my apprehension to move forward in areas of my life. The bolded sentence above for me, is the power that catapulted my mindset shift.

The focus here about when you shine, you give others permission to do so in their own life takes the consciousness off of yourself, your inhibitions, your feelings of inadequacy, your fear and places it on the responsibility you have been given to be a light so that others may find their own way. It is all about acceptance. And once I accepted my God given responsibility, I realized that if I don't show up in my best self, someone is missing out and I am part of the problem.

You are here to lead and inspire. You certainly cannot do that in a fearful state of being. Always keep in mind that you are a part of something bigger. Did I scare you even more? It's true. There is a bigger picture here, a grander scheme of things, a purpose. Perspective is everything.

The fear of failure can be cast down by a new belief system. There's a quote by Henry Ford "Whether you think you can or you can't, you are right." When the fear of success is overwhelming, the fear of failure will befriend us. We can become friends with the fear by unconsciously undermining our efforts toward success. This fear makes us reluctant to try or move forward in the event, just in case we end up 'failing'. Are you living in "just in case" neighborhood of failure?

Do not underestimate the fear of failure. It can lead mental illness in the form of anxiety disorder, depression or obsessive compulsive disorder. Now this bold spirit compounded into other areas to keep you even more crippled and trapped.

We mentioned earlier that when the emotion of fear released, it is sometimes connected to a traumatic experience. When we feel fear, it might induce the experience of a prior trauma and therefore prevent from wanting to go forward. For example, when I was child, all three of my dogs died by the time I was 8. To the day, between my husband and my three children, I a the only one that has no desire to have a family dog.

It is very possible that having a dog in the home w increase my fear of what might happen if I get attache to a family pet that could possibly be "taken away" fro me again. It is interesting to note here that if we do n deal with the fears of our childhood, we could very we take them into our adulthood. The alarming fact is by th time you're an adult, this bold spirit has come int maturation and possibly even a monster that you w have to be determined to destroy in order to live liberty.

The simple truth is, we all have varying definitions success and failure because we all have different goal belief systems, values or benchmarks. It is imperative tha you take time to define what each means to yo

54

personally. This will aid to drown out inaccurate belief systems and the racket of OPP when we have confidence in what works for our own life.

What about Phobias?

You understand to respond in fear is common and even normal. However, a phobia is not mild or moderate fear. It is an anxiety that will literally interfere with a person's ability to function and even their quality of life might be severely affected.

Spending time to make large efforts to avoid something is a phobia. If you have to make arrangements to rearrange your entire day, in order to avoid contact with something, you have a phobia. When you move in extreme and unnecessary patterns to evade interactions, a phobia is most likely.

Nothing and no one should impair your life in such a way that you cannot function to carry out your divine, individual purpose from day to day. This is just another tactic, scheme and strategy straight from the enemy's camp. Do not remain in a powerless frame of thinking.

You should absolutely be seeking professional help for a spiritual breakthrough. It may take multiple times and multiple sources for this disorder to improve, in order for you to thrive the way you need to. What I have realized about healing for wholeness, is that it is never a rushed process or procedure. However, taking your time and moving toward the necessary direction is setting you

up for success emotionally, physically, mentally ar
spiritually.

Conquering Fear

Fear is just information. If that's the case, you need
take the time necessary to educate yourself about th
thing that you are afraid of. Once you have th
knowledge, everything becomes clear and easier as yc
move in the direction to conquer it. However, dor
waste precious time in a state of gathering. Eventua
you must apply the knowledge and face the darn thir
armored with this new data.

Without a doubt, the most effective way to conquer fe
is to have a faceoff with it. What's everyone's favori
quote? "Feel the fear and do it anyway". The fear mc
never go away. But I promise you once you do the thir
that you are fearful of, more than likely you will realiz
that it wasn't as bad as you thought. Remember me c
the roller coaster?

I also found out that fear is a bully. It wants to keep yc
bound and limit your experiences. You have to stand u
to this monster and get to the other side of the very thir
you fear. Now don't get me wrong, some fear is valic
And if we didn't have this emotion within us, we wou
place ourselves in real danger many times.

There are times when fear will save you from preser
danger. Fear is an indication that a possible threat is nec
So it makes you aware and puts you on aler

But once you are in contact with the danger, what's your next step? You must decide if you're going to fight, flee or freeze. A healthy mindset will help you decide the best action to take.

You cannot conquer the bold spirit of fear by harboring negative thoughts in your mind or giving space to negative thoughts by others. Fear thrives on negativity. If you continue to talk yourself out of something long enough, you will soon realize that you don't need to talk anymore. You have now been made a believer of the negative statements that came out of your mouth.

Speak the word of God in the very face of fear. It must submit to His word and if you program your mind to declare God's word over your life, fear has to succumb to it. Likewise, we must combat the negative energy, opinions and words of others by speaking the word!

My eight year old son just helped me write this next paragraph. He and I are home alone and he says "Mom! There's a bee in the house." I looked up from typing and on his face I immediately detected fear (and anger if you know my son. He was ready to fight against this imposter of a bee. How dare this bee come into his space?).

I said "Roc, it's okay. We can get it. Be calm." His face softened as he uttered the next words which were so powerful to me "If you're calm, it won't sting." And with that new information he went back to whatever he was doing.

Yes, if you're calm, it won't sting. Many times we cc puncture the intentions of the bold spirit of fear b counteracting it with a calm spirit. Fear will be rendere powerless once it realizes it doesn't have a victim sting. So the next time this emotion rises up in you, thir "Calm First." You'll immediately take the "sting" out it. And you can thank my son for that insight when yc see him. Thanks son.

In one of my previous corporate settings, a colleagu once told me that my energy is so calm that if th building was on fire, I would be the one that they wou want to be stuck with. I may not always succeed, bu have learned that 'calm first' is the best way to increas clarity and lower anxiety. I've since had enoug alarming experiences, crazy encounters, traumat events to understand the power of calm. Feel, breat deal. That is the formula to calm. Try that next time.

Cut yourself some slack. If you do something or t something new, there is a chance you will experienc the fear of failure. But it only remains a "failure" if yc didn't learn from the experience. Tell yourself, whethe lose or win, I learn. Therefore I will never fail. If what yc learned is truly of value and you apply what you hav learned, this will remain true.

What Does the Bible Say about Fear?

"God has not given us the spirit of fear but of power and of love and of a sound mind." 2 Timothy 1:7.

This is one of the most popular scriptures that comes to mind when we mention fear and one that needs to be rehearsed out loud and in the face of any present danger we face. Fear is not a gift from God. It is quite the opposite as God has "... given us power, love and a sound mind."

Repeat it out loud. Ready? *"God has not given me the spirit of fear. He has given me power, love and a sound mind."* Say until your believe it because it is the truth. The authority of the Word desires to impact your situation but it's waiting for your belief system to catch up and your mouth to make it known in the atmosphere.

When I think of fear in the bible, I immediately go to the disciple Peter and how he walked on water. Did you catch that? Peter walked on water. According to the book of St. Matthew 14:22-33 The disciples were in a boat and they saw a shadow of a person a far off as if walking on the water. Fear immediately gripped their heart. Jesus knowing that they were overcome with fear reassured them that it was Him.

Well the disciples, especially Peter did not believe it. So Peter boldly pipes up "Lord, if it's really you out there, command me to come to you on the water." Now I'm not sure if Peter knew what he was saying initially because in this scenario, there was only one way to get

to Jesus and that was by the same water Jesus w(
walking on.

Jesus bids Peter to "Come." Peter got out of the bo(
and went toward Jesus, meaning Peter was actual
walking on water as well!!! What a miracle for Peter ar
all the disciples that were witnessing this! Peter was s
overcome with shock that he was doing the human
impossible act of actually walking on water.

But he took his eyes off of Jesus, when the winds becam
boisterous and Peter began to sink because he w(
afraid. He took his eyes off Jesus because of FEAR. Her
he was walking on water like Jesus but he allowed th
elements to distract him and he began to sink as humai
will when they try to walk on water on their own. So Pet
called out to Jesus for help and of course, to his rescu
Jesus came.

There are so many nuggets here in this story. But the mo
one is that Peter probably felt the fear and got out of th
boat any way. If he had thought about it too long, th
bold spirit of fear would be too overpowering. Many (
you just need to get out of the boat. Go experience yo
miracle that's waiting for you to make that move.

The other portion is, don't take your eyes off of Jesus. I
Jesus who will aid and support your human limitation k
applying His supernatural power for you to experienc
the wonders awaiting the activation of your faith. If yc
take your eyes off of Him and begin to humanly asse
exactly what is happening, you'll sink quicker than yo
curiosity is able to sustain. This is a word for those wh

need to make haste in giving God the glory for all of their accomplishments. It's not you. It's the God in you.

Scriptures Regarding fear

Joshua 1:9 Have I not Commanded you? Be Strong and courageous. Don't be terrified, don't be discouraged In the Lord your God will be with you, wherever you go.

Isaiah 35:4 " Tell everyone who is discouraged, Be Strong and dont be afraid God is coming to your cue.

Psalms 27:1 " The Lord is my light and my Salvation whom shall fear. The Lord is ~~the~~ ~~my~~ Stronghold 2 my life of whom shall I be afraid:

Psalm 46:1 God is our Refuge and Strength, an ever present help n trouble:

Psalms 118: 6-7 " The Lord is with me I will t be afraid. What 61 can man do to me? e Lord is with me; He is my helper.

Scriptures on Fear Continued

Deuteronomy 31:8

He will never leave you or forsake you. Do not be afraid; do not be discouraged.

Romans 8:28

Isaiah 43:1 " Don't Fear for I have redeemed you; I have called you by my name.

1 John 4:18 " perfect love cast out Fear.

Psalm 18:2 The Lord is my Rock, my fortress and my deliverer.

Isaiah 41:10 So do not fear for I am with you. I am your God. I will strengthen you and help you. I will uphold you with my righteous hand.

Psalm 56:3 when I am afraid I put my trust in you.

Psalm 23:4 Even though I walk through the valley of the Shadow 62 of death I will FEAR NO EVIL.

The Spirit of Pride

*jealousy. intimidation. fear. **pride.** anger.*

Wikipedia says that pride as an inward emotion, has two meanings. In a positive sense, pride is when you are humble and content within yourself with what you have or towards what another person has in such a way that you are able to freely offer them praise, while remaining fulfilled yourself. It is the very essence of being happy with who you are or what you have.

In other context and for the purposes of highlighting this bold spirit, negatively speaking, pride is a *"foolishly and irrationally corrupt sense of one's personal value, status or accomplishments."* As pointed out, St. Augustine says pride is *"the love of one's own excellence."* It is self idolatry manifested in its highest form or an exaggerated self esteem.

You might've heard of the Seven Deadly Sins. Pride is included on that list and it is to be noted that pride is the original sin because all sin stems from a spirit of pride. The bold spirit of pride is dangerous because where pride exists, space for God is extinct. One who possesses the spirit of pride cannot possibly see God as the source if they believe they are the one in control of every outcome and turnout of their lives.

Pride is the one spirit that explicitly states in the Bible, God hates. In I Peter 5:5 *"God opposes the proud but gives grace to the humble."* The word used for opposed means being at war with, in the Greek. If we're at war with God, who do you think is going to win? In essence pride says I want to and I will take the place of God.

I've heard people say and pray "I want to be humble. Maybe they are misinformed. You don't want God to humble you, although He can, He will and He does at times. The appropriate prayer is "God, help me to be humble." Help me to never forget that you are my ultimate Source.

It's in Him we live. It's in Him we move. It's in Him we have our being. We might as well not move at all, unless we move in Him. In contradiction, the spirit of pride causes one to become comfortable in a delusional state of security.

It is no wonder that the letter "I" is right smack in the middle of the word pride. This bold spirit of pride is led by "me, myself and pride" and is very close to its cousin EGO, which is essentially Edging. God. Out. Pride deals with security and ability and the over estimation of one's capability in both.

Here is why pride is also dangerous. When you are prideful, you will lose the very things that you are prideful about. It's best to adapt a spirit of humility and gratitude. I once heard someone say that grateful people know how to keep their blessings and it's true. When you are grateful, you understand that you were chosen out of many. When you are full of pride, you believe that you are entitled above any.

Am I Prideful?

We are not challenging a healthy dose of confidence here. We are exposing motives of the heart. So you must ask ourselves the hard questions. Where do your true intentions lie, when you make every effort to be seen in a positive light? Is it for self glory, to show that you are above everyone else? If this is your preoccupation, then you are full of the bold spirit of pride.

Do you acknowledge God for all of your success and in all that you do? God needs to have the right position in your life, as the head, or you will get the tail end of the deal. This means, going through the process of humiliation and/or being humbled by Him.

If you look down on others and never look up to God, the bold spirit of pride resides within you. Looking down on others because you esteem your own success, possessions and even righteousness is in direct conflict with the heart of God. There is no favoritism with God and no partiality. We are all equally His workmanship and your showmanship is stealing God's shine.

Boasting, sharing or telling your good works to make others seem less worthy, is an act of pride as well. In biblical context, The Pharisees and the Sadducees were known to make their works known and shown in the public arena, by praying aloud and exploiting their good deeds for the spotlight. Their hearts were full of pride.

Did you know that you insult God when you mock thos who are less fortunate, less educated, less skillful tha you? You cannot look down on others because eve single thing that you have, was *given* to you. Oh, I kno you may have worked hard for it. You may hav inherited it. It is very possible it's innate for you to do wh you do. But realize that what you have received can ju as easily be taken away. Let not the bold spirit of pric be the cause of that.

Let me note here that there are many who are indee gifted, talented and capable, seemingly almc effortlessly. And sometimes those who may not be, cc look down on those who are and come to th conclusion that they are prideful. Excellence is not a si More on that later.

When an individual embodies the spirit of pride, the detest the truth. It is no wonder that the father of lies (th enemy) hates the truth. See, the truth about a perso place or thing can be very humbling. Some would muc rather live a lie, than face the truth of their actior behavior and even their thoughts.

I will leave you with this "*Not that we are not sufficient ourselves to think of anything as being from ourselve but our sufficiency is from God.*" 2 Corinthians 3:5

False Pride

If pride is present, I hope that your heart will be softene as the mind is made aware. However, false pride cc lead to a definitive mindset and lifestyle that tells you that you don't need to change because you are perfect just the way you are.

This is a slippery slope because life is about growing and evolving. False pride is a hardened heart towards God and humanity. It doesn't allow you the opportunity to *"grow in grace and in the knowledge of Jesus Christ. To Him be glory both now and forever. Amen."* 2 Peter 3:18. Be careful that you are not living in false pride.

As was mentioned in one article, false pride is like mental alcohol. When one is drunk, in reality they have lost control. They won't get very far before they tumble or disaster strikes. It is the same with a person living in false pride. Eventually, they will succumb to the illness of an uncontrolled ego.

Below are a few examples. Of course please note that the following is what flows *consistently* from a heart that lives in false pride.

"I'm so humble."

The first sign that someone is not humble is the fact that they constantly express that they are.

"I'm so busy."

This is for those that pretend to be interested in your world, but they are super self absorbed in their own. You must take the time to check in on others, especially those you love, no matter what's going on in your world. And taking the time to be 'present' when in the presence of others is key to relationship growth.

"You Can't Tell Me Anything."

If you're willing, you learn something every day. Eve better, if you're open, you can learn from others. Yo can especially learn from those who you believe kno more than you but just the same, being inspired by th most unlikely person is a lesson in and of itself.

Stay open minded around those from different culture belief system, ethnicities that are outside of your norr This is not to say that you should adjust your value standards and boundaries. Use your grain of salt ar proceed.

Sometimes we may not want to receive a rebuke correction much less from those "not on our level." E aware that those we deem "lower" than us, can also se things in us that needs improvement. Listening can he you grow faster than blocking, belittling and battlir against honest conversations, ever will.

Also for consideration is if you get upset or angry when conversation is not going your way, you are walking false pride. You do have to agree to disagree at time Know when to hold your peace and when it's n necessary for you to prove your point.

"I'm Modest."

Have you ever noticed that the more money som people earn, is the better they treat themselves or th nicer the things they have? Yes, there are also peop that are rich but you would never guess based on ho frugal they are with their earnings.

However, consider your words when you continually declare how modest you are. Could it be possible that you are excessively modest due to belittling yourself around others because you do feel unworthy or useless? Or perhaps, you participate in this kind of language as a way not to bring attention to yourself?

"I'm Quiet,"

I'm not certain where I first heard the quote "a *quiet river runs deep*." And it is so true. Those that are quiet may only be "quiet" around you. I've realized that silence is louder than noise. So you don't have to broadcast your disposition, it is already "speaking" for itself.

And are you being quiet because you are timid, afraid to speak up, think your point will not be received or is valid? There is a difference between speaking up when it counts and laying low in fear.

"I Don't Care What People Think."

This statement must be the most famous of statements laced in false pride. I. Don't. Care. What. People. Think. Teenagers say it and adults definitely have rehearsed this kind of response as well. Can I share something with you? Come a little closer. Closer. EVERYONE CARES TO A CERTAIN DEGREE WHAT PEOPLE THINK.

Let's define care. It's not that you will necessarily place your life on hold until people change their opinions of you. However, if this is your constant declaration and response to rightful correction, positive feedback, or constructive criticism, you guessed it, you are practicing a false sense of pride.

When you are humble, you will find it easier to receive feedback, criticism and correction, because your entire mindset is toward growing. How will you grow unless you know?

"I'm Fine."

Now this one, I have to be honest, I often engage in. You may catch me on any given day, just like the rest of humanity telling someone I'm fine, when I may not be doing fine at all. We know that it can be a superficial answer to avoid, cover up and hide what may really be happening in our heart, mind and lives.

Since most of us engage in that response and it is societal norm, I want us to just take a minute to do a self check that we're being honest in our response and more importantly to those who genuinely care for our well being. At the same token, you cannot share with everybody when you have not the slightest clue what they will do with the information. I do believe however, when we participate in sharing ourselves authentically, our stories, our journey, our lives will inspire others to do the same.

The Glorification of Victimization

Criminals usually blame their victims. At the same token, victims need to stop blaming themselves, rehearsing the trauma and regurgitating the experience. If you are not careful, you are practicing false sense of humility and walking in pride, by using what happened to you as a way to seek sympathy, pity or even praise "being a survivor".

You cannot glorify your traumas and negative experiences by continually drawing attention to yourself by way of highlighting the experience every opportunity you get. This is not to downplay what happened. But it is to get you to a point where you stop identifying with the negative occurrence in conversation, in mindset and especially through your lifestyle.

When you share your story, try to ensure that it is the right time and place to do so. It doesn't hurt to also make certain that you are edifying others and not consistently looking for sympathy, a way to connect or to garner unnecessary attention to you and yours. You may find a few who care. But most people love a great, positive ending. And if you are still processing through it all, that's okay as well. We all heal differently. Just ensure that you are indeed on a path to become whole.

Pride in Action

As with any emotion, it is near impossible to be prideful and not express it. The body language can include a tilt back of the head, slightly inflated chest, hands on the hips. Some people don't know how to hide their prideful spirit. It is written all over their body language.

Understand that this could be a turnoff not just for others but also for God. God may decide to make an example out of you. And not the kind that you think. Be humble heart and your actions will follow.

Overcoming Pride

Disobedience is at the root of pride. When you do n obey the truth, you walk in pride so that your flesh cc be comfortable with the lie you've been telling yourse The more you tell yourself a lie is the more you will believ the lie, until eventually you become the lie, which now your skewed truth.

If you're ever going to overcome pride, you must ge back to basics. Turn your entire heart over to God. Th reason why it's your heart that you need to turn over Him first is because "*the heart is deceitful (it lies) abov all things and desperately wicked; who can know it?..* Jeremiah 17:9 When confronted with the truth, peop often say "Well, God knows my heart." And that is th truth. However, you may be able to trick ar camouflage to man, but not to God. He does know th intent of each heart.

Remain humble. Just keep God at the center of it c You might forget or lose sight from time to time. G back on track so you don't completely lose your way. you ever feel the slightest urge that you are lookir down on others or exalting your works without givir God the glory, know that the bold spirit of pride is lurkir somewhere. Know to cast it down immediatel

What about Ego?

I have already mentioned that the first cousin of pride is ego. Let's go there for a minute.

Ego can be likened to self respect in a positive way in that it aids you as you fulfill your life's purpose. In a negative sense, an unhealthy ego is you separating yourself from God. And here is why that doesn't work.

Once you separate yourself and take your life into your own hands, you will in enough time realize that without Him, you can do nothing. So why take the unnecessary trip? Soon you'll be right back where you started anyway.

Do you believe that you can save everybody yourself?

Do you lie about your life experiences in order to prove that all is well?

Do you hold your spirituality in such high regard that you look down on others that are less spiritual than you?

Are you so adamant about your walk with Christ being perfect that you debate instead of conversing on matters that you don't agree with?
If so, then you may have Edging God Out syndrome. (EGO). To reset your ego in a healthy way is to ensure that all of your life's decisions and choices are leading in the direction they should be. Serve others and be selfless in your serving Qualify everything you do to make certain you have the proper intent and mindset about it in its purest form. Watch how you affect others and

ensure you are treating them in love and with kindness.

I love this Arab poem:

The words of the tongue have three gatekeepers.

Before words get past the lips, the first gatekeeper ask
"Is this true?" That stops a lot of traffic immediately. But
the words get past the first gatekeeper, there is a secor
who asks, "Is it kind?" And for those words that quali
here too, the last gatekeeper asks, "Is it necessary?"

Is this true? Is it kind? Is it necessary? This is certair
a formula for a healthy mind, a healthy soul, a healtr
spirit and a healthy body.

What Does the Bible Say about Pride?

First of all, God hates pride because in its basic form,
promotes independence (from Him) and rebellic
(against Him).

"In his pride the wicked does not seek Him; in all h
thoughts there is no room for God." Psalm 10:4 NIV

Secondly, pride permeates a hardened heart (towarc
Him). There's not much that God can do with that.

The most familiar scenario of pride in its most compellir
way is the story of King Nebuchadnezzar recorded
Daniel 5. The bible said the king became so ve
arrogant and hardened with pride that God stripped hi
of his throne and glory. Make no mistake that God v
not share His glory with anyone else. Doesn't that mal
sense since no one can do the things that God can do?

Afterward, God actually gave this king a mind of an animal. And he lived with animals including donkeys and ate grass like cows. This kept happening until the King came to his senses and acknowledged that God was the Most High. At the end of the day, that's really what God is looking for, some acknowledgment. How have you taken time in your work, in your words and in your thoughts to acknowledge who is in fact at the helm of your life?

You may need to come to your senses like the prodigal son in Luke 15. He realized that he was better than being downsized to eating what the animals ate. Then he humbled himself and returned to his father's house to ask forgiveness.

It is not uncommon for God to trim your material possessions first so He can get your attention before he gives you over to a way of life you're not going to like. It's better you come to your senses now without needing to have God step in and show you yourself.

The Spirit of Anger

*jealousy. intimidation. fear. pride. **anger.***

Anger. Meet the number one health problem, as documented by a former U.S. Surgeon. Anger is an emotion used without intellect and is sometimes used as a punishment with the intention of causing emotional pain. What is important here is not that the emotion is not normal. It is both normal and common. However when it processes, it is void of common sense and the ability to reason.

The Bible says *"Be Angry and do not sin."* Ephesians 4:26 It is what we do with the anger that causes sin to be present in our life. Anger is so common that it has no qualms about affecting communities, relationships and even your individual health. When anger is unresolved it can become a residing spirit.

It is triggered by unforgiveness, regret or even guilt. In other words, this bold spirit of anger surfaces due to unresolved experiences that trigger within us without warning. The bold spirit of anger is deep, deep bitterness towards the person who you feel is responsible for the pain you are experiencing.

Here's the thing, often having a solid conversation can alleviate some of the pain. It would be like taking an aspirin for a headache. The truth of the matter is, that some people would rather live with the headache and normalize it than find a solution to have it disappear.

What also remains true is that you must consider the "some people do not have the mental capacity to b who you need them to be." You may never have th opportunity to have that conversation to resolve th matter, the issue or bring mutual understanding of th experience. This is when forgiving yourself and releasir your own guilt, matters the most.

How to Identify the Spirit of Anger

Do you blow a fuse when corrected or redirected due your own error or misstep?

Do you despise the bond formed by a former friend ar a mutual friend?

Do you hold people to a high standard, even high than the standard you have for yourself and fe immense disappointment when they don't meet yo criteria?

Do you feel life has treated you unfairly as you glance your neighbor's success and feel envious of them eve though they are oblivious to your feelings?

Do you marginalize everyone based on your negativ experience with one or a few?

Did you once feel a great deal of pride in one area b after failing more than once in the same area, you a now angry with yourself for not being who you onc were?

Are people on edge around you?

Is there a topic of conversation that automatically sets you off?

Does the mention of a person's name cause you blow a fuse even when you are outside of their presence?

If you can attest to any of the above, it might be safe to say that the bold spirit of anger is resident in your heart.

Humans are flawed. There I said it. I know it. I own it. Why? Because I am human and I am flawed. This was a conversation I had with my therapist during one of our sessions. It helped me realize that as much as I'd like to hope to be all that I'm supposed to be, I am about as flawed as the next person. And the next person is about as flawed as me.

I recall sitting in the audience at an event when the very high profile and known individual who was being interviewed opened up the floor for Q & A from the attendees. One attendee sitting on the front brought up a very controversial topic and asked this well known person what was their position on the subject matter. It might've been to bring clarity, to expose the person as a fraud or flawed human or this was the attendee's way of needing her anger addressed.

I liked and will never forget what the special guest said in answer, "*Please allow me the same grace for understanding your position as I allow you the grace to stand in your position.*" This is what we must remember no stand in that position." This is what we must remember no matter how difficult. Let's approach one another with grace, first. Let's speak to one another in grace. Let remember that it's grace that has brought us all this far and grace will help us to complete our journey.

Eph. 4:31-32 *"Let all bitterness, and wrath and anger and clamor and evil speaking be put away from you, with malice: and be ye kind one to another, tenderhearted forgiving one another, even as God for Christ's sake has forgiven you."*

Do You Have a Right to Be Angry?

Plain and simple, some stuff just hurts! Traumatic events and negative experiences can change the trajectory our lives. There are countless stories of being a victim offense, abuse and violence that were certainly not our fault.

We have to remember that *"Vengeance is mine, said the Lord. I will repay."* Deuteronomy 32:35. I've seen God fight more battles on my behalf than I ever could if I had uttered a word or put up my dukes. I love the verse that says *"When the enemy comes in like a flood, the spirit the Lord will lift up a standard against him."* Isaiah 59: Yes, there is a standard set. And when the enemy cross that barrier, he has hell to pay, literally.

Anger might be used to justify injustice. And rightfully so However, a closer look reveals that there will be occasions that you will want to be angered, but don get angry. Why not get angry? Well, once you've gotten angry, sinning, wrongdoing, a misstep, a mistake, one wrong move is just around the corner. Don't even put yourself in that position. Move out of the way of anger.

Have you ever seen an angry man, woman or child? Let me rephrase that. Anyone that allows or has the bold spirit of anger to rise up in them, will assuredly act, behave, speak and even look different from what is their normal disposition.

Don't you think for one minute that people will get away with their wrong doing. It use to make me very upset, ticked off and ready to fight whenever I would think about all the people that have seemingly gotten away after they have left me wounded, bleeding, hurt and disappointed. To be honest, those feelings may still try to rise up within me from time to time.

But after self composure, I remember that God knows how to handle everything and everybody quite well. I may never even be around to see just how it's handled, or how God "gets them back". And really, it's none of my business.

The only thing we have to hold on to is His word that promises a day of reckoning. When God blesses you in front of your enemies the point is for them to see you doing better, bigger and brighter. Not bitter, depressed and wounded. Let God take charge of your heart as well as deal with them accordingly. Believe me, He can do both at the same time.

Our country is currently trying to deal with anger ar
through organizations like the Black Lives Matt
movement, and those who support it, justifiably so. Ju
recently, another officer was acquitted in the death
another unarmed black man by a white police offic
who claimed he was fearful for his life and so he sh
rounds on the black man.

You can see just how upsetting it is with the habit
injustice in our court system and with counterpar
outside of the black culture would be. So what to c
with that anger? Press conferences. March. Rallie
Retaliate. All of them have happened and the situatic
seemingly worsened.

To this I concede with an article on the website of Hom
School Digest that clarified the difference betwee
fighting for what is right and personal vengeance. Whe
you're angry you will place that spirit in the wrong are
even if the area is closely linked to the source of injustic
indifference and intolerance.

When you fight for what is right, you rally for a cause. Yc
create solutions, you don't highlight problems. You c
not rest until laws are changed, through voting, speakir
up, showing up and being a presence in full force ur
change is made.

When you have a personal vengeance, then yo
feelings are all in whatever your cause is. And the thir
about feelings like Myleik Teele, one of my favori
podcasters says is feelings? Well, they just aren't fac

Feelings come and go. They carry you but you can't depend on them to lead you down the right path. Feelings fill you but they don't feed you. They pull you but they don't position you for the long haul all the time. A direct choice must be made to fight for what is right, what is just, what is correct whether our personal feelings are attached to it or not.

The same article pointed out that it is easier to use anger as a substitute for study. You might say, "Study? Who wants to study?! Let's handle this now. We don't have time for study." A spirit of anger cannot be used in the presentation of truth.

I think of a past conversation I had with one of my daughters. She reluctantly told me that she had done something her dad and I had previously asked her not to do. In retrospect, I was so angry about what she had done for a second time, rather than teaching her the principles of obedience.

As I began to unleash my passion and tried to convey to her my feelings, I realized that my anger had taken over, even though you couldn't convince me that I was not presenting a case on behalf of God, to keep her out of trouble.

I even used words I would not have used in everyday conversation. But I was angry. Did she hear me? Oh yes, loud and clear. But how appropriately did I present the truth of the matter instead of the passion of anger in the moment?

As I think about it, not very well. I thought of everythir as I launched, including manipulation mixed with th word of God. And a raised voice coupled with wic eyes hoping that she'd get my point, emphatically.

I'm hoping that the truth was not lost in all the noise. B instead, I should've presented the truth, pray to God c her behalf and left it in the hands of the Lord. Those a the steps that I must take, if I want to see the sovereign of God made manifest in real time.

And what about controlled anger? You know, the kir that isn't unleashed all at once or the kind that directed elsewhere as in screaming in a pillow or as recommended, counting to 10. I'm not going to try fool you. I have participated in these. And I may hav felt a release in that moment but ultimately I believe th my anger was only subsided. I'm sure it showed up other areas later.

Anger is an emotion that can be controlled by the tru of God's Word and telling your mind to redirect thoughts so that your actions manifest the truth of wha in God's word. No one wants to talk about what th should look like, perhaps because it's boring or it tak too much effort on our part.

Well, for those of you who are serious about controllir your anger God's way, here it is. We are commissione to show love, joy, peace, longsuffering, gentlene goodness, faith, meekness and temperance. If you find hard to exude any of those, you must make an effort surrender to the process. Please note that you cannot accomplish this on your own. You must seek a higher power to enable you to exhibit what you were designed to showcase.

The Bible says that Moses, as a young man saw an Egyptian beating an Israelite. Moses got angry and killed the Egyptian. That is the first account of Moses' anger but not the last. In fact, as one of the greatest biblical leaders, Moses' anger would be documented up to at least 10 more times.

Let the record show, and it does, that Moses was not allowed to enter the promised land of Canaan because he permitted anger to get the best of him. What are you angry about that has prevented you from receiving God's best for you?

The Cause of Anger

Did you know that the root cause of anger is from tension that is pent up? Whether you realize it or not, everyday you're building on something. Is it a sinking sand or is it a solid foundation? You can build with the wrong materials if you like, but eventually your spiritual, physical, emotional house will come crashing down.

Another thing to keep in mind is, we've all heard the saying "*hurting people, hurt people*." Well, usually "*angry people, come from angry families*". You have to watch what negative influences are now upon you that are imbedded in your own family.

Family means familiar. So for example, the bold spirit anger may be so familiar to your family that you are n even aware of its existence or the influence in your ow heart and behavior. This is your time to brec generational curses and strongholds within your fam' that also need to be uprooted in your own life. Here's closing thought, "*healed people, heal people.*"

Anger Management

Step away. Step away. The Bible does admonish us "*be slow to wrath.*" James 1:19. I wonder how mar times we could've avoided getting angry or giving in anger if we had just stepped away from anger « together? And I do mean physically and emotionally.

I hear somebody saying "*Don't start nothin', won't b nothin'*" or "*I won't start it, but if you bring it, it's on.*" ar "*I don't start fights but I'll finish them.*" Disengac people. That is where your power lies. Getting ang even to the point of violence shows how powerful th other party has control over your emotions and just hc much you need to build up your own mental frame.

You really should acknowledge that you are carrying th bold spirit of anger immediately! First admit it to God ar if the occasion calls for it to a mentor or a spiritual guic who can walk you through the process of releasin Releasing anger has a lot to do with unforgiveness. you're still trying to justify your anger, then you a probably not ready to release your internal anger.

Should you have the opportunity to have the difficult conversation(s), listen more than you speak. Listen to understand, not to prove your point or justify your behavior. And most importantly, ask for forgiveness. Be mindful that the other party may not be ready to forgive you. Again, that is none of your business. This is a matter of the heart. You are ensuring that you are in right standing with God.

During another one of our sessions, my therapist mentioned that by nature, we tend to let things build up and build up instead of dealing with them as they arise. What then happens is, we explode because there has been such an increase of tension within the body, that as fragile as our bodies are, it does not have the capacity to contain it all.

This is partly what happened to me in the fall of 2016. I began the beginning of that year so disappointed and confused about a particular situation. Month after month, I would share with just my family but unknowingly tension was building up in my body. I was angry. I was bewildered. I was headed toward much bitterness as feelings of helplessness eroded all around me.

By mid-October I had reached out to one other person. I didn't share all the details but that conversation only put things into perspective. It didn't give me an action plan of how to deal with my feelings.

Sure enough, I felt what I would describe as, a fist on my chest. It began that Monday evening and lasted until

Saturday morning. Throughout that week, I proceede
with life as usual including my 9-5, wife dutie
motherhood mode, entrepreneurial passions...

On the morning of October 15th, my heart had begun
palpitate, hard and fast. My heart. My poor hea
Doctors said that my heart had beat so fast, hard and f
so long that I had bruised the lining of my heart ar
released acid into my blood stream.

Doctors also mentioned that my heart was beating
rapidly, it was as if I had been running sprints like a trac
star. Being a track mom and my family being a trac
family, I definitely could relate at how much of c
concern this was.

Thank God I was able to come out alive from th
traumatic experience. I began to exercise more. I dra
my green smoothies. I tried to become more physica
active. I stretched more. I breathed deeper and longer

I tried not to raise my voice as much. I tried to remo
calm whenever possible. Most importantly, I released n
own self from spaces, places and obligations that r
longer served my heart in a healthy way. I embrace
self care and it was about time.

It's unfortunate that it had to be a near dea
experience for me to realize that allowing feelings ar
the spirit of anger stemming from being severe
disappointed to take root, kills you softly than a
individual or the experience my anger was directe
toward.

88

However, I'm grateful I can now share my story and hopefully save lives as I continually save my own.

It's a process. Some days my heart feels right. At other times, I have to nurture it more. But all days, I place myself in the Master's Hand and take care of my needs, emotionally and mentally. Oh and self care? It's not selfish, it's necessary. When you deal with the spirit of anger in a healthy way, it will definitely build your character and decrease your need for validation.

On another note, are your expectations of others too high? See disappointment will leave the door open for the bold spirit of anger to come in. When you remember that humans are flawed, just as you are, you're able to maintain the right amount of dosage needed to place everyone in their rightful position in your life.

Stop yourself from feeling so heavily disappointed. People are going to make mistakes. And release yourself from believing that titles should automatically mean that people have worked on their character as well. The two don't necessarily go hand in hand nor are they always a given.

A person may be disciplined academically but need to work on their communication skills. Someone may have great financial equity but is a horrible confidante. Accept people for where they are, who they are and deal with them accordingly. I think Maya Angelou said it best. "When people show you who they are, believe them."...the first time.

What Does the Bible Say about the Spirit of Anger?

According to Jonah 4:4,9 the prophet Jonah was angry with God because he wanted God to judge his enemies. Isn't that how we sometimes get? You utter "fix it Jesus" but you really mean, "fix them"! I get it. And sometimes I wonder why does it take God so long to "fix people" especially when they have done wrong?!

Back to Jonah...as I contemplate on several instances where I was treated unfairly and I wanted God to come down from heaven and teach a few people here and there a few lessons. I wished that God would get up from His throne and tell them with all power in His hands, take several seats! Ok, is that just me? Maybe, so seriously now, back to Jonah.

Instead God brought a revival and forgave the people. That is not what Jonah expected. So God asked him "Do you have good reason to be angry?" And of course, Jonah insisted that he did, but it was quite obvious he did not.

What if God performed the same wrath on you that you wished on others? The way God deals with people and things is really up to His discretion as He is the One that ultimately knows best. Surely, you would beg for mercy and forgiveness if portions were available for of all your own mistakes and sins.

And I know some are not sorrowful about what they do or have done. They continue to remain in God's hands and he will "downsize" them in their due season.

It may not be how you would do it. It may not be in your timing. But God always circles back.

There was also a man in the Bible named Haman who was full of pride but he had a very high position in the Persian Kingdom. As he stood at the King's gate, mere noble men who saw him would quickly bow in respect. Well, one man name Mordecai refused to bow. Can you imagine how angry that made Haman?

Haman didn't just ignore it and move on. I mean, if one person doesn't bow down to you does that take away from your position in the Kingdom? That's food for thought. However, Haman did not ignore Mordecai but instead became very angry. He was so angry that he began to plot the death of not only Mordecai, a Jewish man, but of all the Jews in the Kingdom. Well, that's going overboard. And anger will do that. It will throw you overboard.

Guess who ended up dying by the very trap he set for others? Sure enough, Haman was hanged by the gallows that had originally been built to hang Mordecai. Let people hang themselves. Don't let your anger over what people have done or may be doing to you, cause you to be hung first or instead.

When the Spirits Connect and Collaborate

jealousy. intimidation. fear. pride. anger.

All of the five bold spirits, **jealousy, intimidation, fear, pride** and **anger** are extremely contagious. I want you to read that like it's a disease, a deadly, common disease. For in actuality if they are allowed to be alive through you, they will kill the spirit of God within you.

Each bold spirit doesn't want to stand alone and thus invites and welcomes other spirits to help in the mission of destruction. Among the five bold spirits, you may also find, envy, covetousness, malice, hate and lust to name a few. We certainly don't want to leave out gossiping, judging, criticizing, backbiting and lying just to name a few more. It will be in one person, jump on the next person and still can come through another individual.

The evidence can be seen in what has been the demolition of families, relationships, churches, organizations and business. I dare say what lies beneath the aftermath of each of these, would be tied to the main content of this book; The Five Bold Spirits. I don't want you to ever forget them, *jealousy, intimidation, fear, pride* and *anger.*

It's usually a combination, collaboration or a collision of all. If not confronted and dealt with, it will pass from generation to generation. It can begin as a small thing and develop into a big ordeal. This will cause destruction upon destruction.

Since the five bold spirits love to connect with oth
spirits, expect that when a person is carrying *eith*
jealousy, intimidation, fear, pride or **anger** they will se
or be attracted to other individuals who house the sam
First, it will be for the sake of validating their thoughts ar
possibly even to carry out their destructive behavior. B
more so, the enemy uses this kind of collaboration
accomplish his mission (to steal, kill and destroy) quick
and more efficiently.

Be careful who you share stories, information or secre
with if you are aware that indeed you have any of th
five bold spirits within you. It needs to be a carefu
chosen mentor, an experienced accountability partn
a well tried, true and trusted source. If not, then wh
happens is, you will be used by the enemy to continue
fulfill his agenda against your sister or brother. This is n
to be taken lightly, especially when you *are* the sister
brother.

You'll know you have shared with the wrong perso
when they have joined in with you instead of telling yo
the truth at the risk of dissolving whatever relationsh
you have with them. You'll know this person is not of Go
when they make it even bigger than how you presente
it, or they add negative information you didn't even a
for.

You'll know you have shared with the wrong perso
when all you wanted to do was share, but they want
act out in violence instead. You'll know you have share
with the wrong person when you attempt to move towo

positivity but they keep stirring up negativity.

It's collaboration and not the kind you want to engage in. This kind is deadly for you and for those involved. It's deadly for your spirit. Cease and abort mission, immediately.

You've heard the saying that opposites attract. Well, I use to believe that wholeheartedly. Not so much now. The other day I posted on Facebook the following meme *"Some people are only "attracted" to each other because their demons know each other."*

Having that post be shared at least 36 times was the greatest amount of shares I have ever had, but I knew that a nerve was struck. Perhaps it was people acknowledging their own demons, because believe me we all have something we're struggling with. Or maybe it resonated so much because people were realizing that birds of a feather really do flock together. I'm certain you've heard the saying, *"Show me your friends and I'll tell you who you are."* And this one, *"You know a tree by the fruit it bears."*

Start paying attention to your relationships more closely. I'm certain you'll find a theme, a thread, a connection running through that binds them together for good or evil. Additionally, keep your eyes wide open, or stay woke as they say, when people want to, try to and have connected with you in some form or fashion.

Ask yourself, *"Have they entered my space to highlight my weakness or will they enhance my good work?"*

The key here is hopefully you're already flowing in yo destiny. Because, if there is anything that the enen loves is an idle mind, an open heart and a bored life. TI is his playing field. So stay productive and effective, n just busy.

Watch those that seemingly come out of nowhere. B all of a sudden they are your biggest fan and yo loudest cheerleader. Now of course, this is not everyor but I've seen it happen so often that I would be amiss didn't expose it. It's amazing how people can see harmless but are really harmful to your spirit.

Learn to stand in your own power always and nev forget who you are at the core. You don't need anyor to validate what is already confirmed inside of yo Praise from anyone is changeable because it's based c how they feel. Respect is what they will have for yc even when they can't fathom why they don't like yc So be careful who and why you invest with your tim your energy, your heart and most importantly, your life.

A Word about Strongholds

jealousy. intimidation. fear. pride. anger.

If all we do is expose the spirits without uncovering strongholds, then we leave the mind gate open for a stronghold to exist in the first place. What are strongholds? The dictionary defines it as *a place that has been fortified so as to protect it against attack* or *a place where a particular cause or belief is strongly defended or upheld.* I wanted to address spiritual strongholds here because it houses and gives The Five Bold Spirits a place of residence to lodge. This place is in the mind, where the battle or move in day begins.

In other words, strongholds are mental habits that are incorrect and contrary to the truth. A stronghold develops when an individual has spent too much time believing a lie. This negative, inward influence affects outward attitude and behavior that develop into patterns of consistency, which now must be broken down. What are your strongholds?

Strongholds thrive in shame based thinking. It occurs when you think of your past hurt and failures and then replay the broken record over and over in your head until you now believe that you are a failure. Broken records produce broken people who live broken lives. This is the reason you must be *mind*ful of what you meditate on. Whatever you meditate on, you create with.

Your mind must now be transformed with a renewed way of thinking. You must speak and believe a new truth which is actually the absolute truth. How do you fight lie? You fight it with the truth. What is the truth? The true is written in God's word. That is where you will find o the truth of who you are and the truth of how God see you and how he desires you to live. It is the knowledge and the application of the truth that sets us free.

One of the most appropriate scripture to reference he is 2 Corinthians 10:3-5 *"For though we walk in the fles we do not war after the flesh: (For the weapons of o warfare are not carnal, but mighty through the pullir down of strongholds;) Casting down imaginations, ar every high thing that exalteth itself against th knowledge of God, and bringing into captivity eve thought to the obedience of Christ."*

If you remember the temptation of Christ in th wilderness, you will note that every time the ener tempted him, Jesus used scripture to counteract every attempt. That is the same strategy we must use ward off the enemies device of using our mind as playground. This is why it is of utmost importance that yc hide the word of God in your heart, and meditate c that which is good.

It is just beneficial to read God's word, meditate on and live in the realm of inspiration, empowerment ar self development. It is not that you won't be tempte but you will become acutely aware of what a lie is ar what the truth is. When you are able to immediately fig off the attacks on your mind, the enemy will have no choice but to leave you, as he did Jesus in the wilderness, even if it's for a season.

For all the guilt, shame and reminders of our failures that the enemy tries to bring up, I reference here a saying that I heard as a little child. "*When the enemy tries to remind you of your past, you must remind him of his future.*" You can't reason with your enemy. You can't ignore him and you certainly must not believe him. What you can do is set your own ambush by blocking and not feeding into his lies.

Armed with the knowledge of what strongholds are, The Five Bold Spirits will only take root if they are allowed to become strongholds. Build up your mental health and spiritual well being. Test the things that run across your mind as to whether they are the absolute truth or not. Do not think on, repeat or meditate on the lie. Cast it down as soon as it appears.

I See You. You See Me.

jealousy. intimidation. fear. pride. anger.

There is no mirror attached to bodies that enables you to see people from the inside out. Can you imagine if you were able to view the thoughts, intents and the content of other people's hearts? Perhaps it would be beneficial and would grant you necessary information on how to deal with them.

Would you become more loving, kind and patient if everyone walked around in a physically vulnerable state? Maybe as a society we would actively be more careful to hide all personal feelings, hang ups and vexations.

On the flip side, if we all had mirrors, there might be some people that would continue to be raw, offensive and abrasive. They might figure, they have nothing to hide and nothing to lose. We can only imagine how it would be.

So although you don't have signs, banners or mirrors, be aware that the content of your heart, the state of your spirit and the condition of your soul, are always on display. You may attempt to hide it, tuck it away or even pretend it doesn't exist but it will always be revealed, even if at first it just seeps out.

The only way to adjust your own vision and perception of others is to remember that as stated before, humans are flawed. In 2 Corinthians 12:7 Paul spoke of a thorn in the flesh for which he could not rid himself of.

I know that everyone has a thorn. Some thorns a
evident to the naked eye because they are expose
Other thorns are not as visible and maybe tha
because a much better job is done of hiding them b
they do exist.

If I have a thorn, a weakness, an impediment
something that I must battle with on a daily basis ar
you experience the same, do you see where we wou
find it more difficult to be so judgmental and cut peop
off and out of our lives? Now I'm not promoting allowir
anyone to consistently abuse you or violate yo
personhood. From those situations, we need God
grace and wisdom to be able to begin a new journey
healing.

However, we do perish for lack of knowledge. Eve
though God's word is packed with promises that app
to every aspect of our lives, we are dying on the insid
and bleeding on the outside because of ignorance
scripture. When you have facts, it is very difficult f
someone to come along and persuade you otherwise.

If you are building your life on the Word of God an
have accepted His written word as if it was His spoke
word, the enemy would not have the ability to ruptu
your heart, wreak as much havoc in your life and pla
seeds of discord with your brothers and sisters.

A new commentary is needed for those who are read
to be vulnerable not to man, but to God. This narrative
found in scripture. There's a dose for every condition th
meets you at the point of your individual need. If you a

ever going to be set free and live free of the bondage of The Five Bold Spirits, His word is what will purify your heart, restrain harmful behavior, reverse thwarted attitudes and clean all "mirrors".

A More Excellent Way

Throughout each page, we have explored with great detail the Five Bold Spirits that exists to ultimately cause inner destruction. I hope you know more now than you did prior to picking up this book and reading the contents. You should be able to clearly discern, identify and disarm **jealousy**, **intimidation**, **fear**, **pride** and **anger**.

But I hear you. Is that it? Now what? Enough already with what we should avoid. What should we seek after? What should we strive for? I for one, don't want to just leave you hanging with great notes, nuggets and notions on how your character might be flawed or to highlight how imperfect we are as humans. Yes, you were given substantial strategy, effective tools and even have become more self aware.

So this is what we should all strive for. If you place your efforts here, you will inadvertently become it. What is it? What should we seek after? What should we strive for? What am I speaking of? Ready? Here it is.

A more excellent way.

Teach me Michelle. Ok, I will.

It's to be more…EXCELLENT.

The Spirit of Excellence is what you should yearn to possess. And I'm here for it. I hope you are as well. I was first introduced to those words "The Spirit of Excellence" by way of Daniel in the Bible. If you've never heard the

bible story of Daniel, cozy up and let's get going her
Daniel 6:3 states *"Then this Daniel was preferred abo*
the presidents and princes, because an excellent sp
was in him.."

Hold on. Daniel was preferred above everyone els
simply because he had an excellent spirit? So wh
strikes me here is there are many capable and skille
people that are in positions but it doesn't mean they a
the preferred one. Just because you are in the positic
does not mean God wants you there or that even othe
want you there, for that matter. Perhaps you are the
simply because of your skill set but not really yc
character.

This also lets me know that there are people that m
not be to the naked eye as good looking, efficient or
popular, and they may have the purest of intentions, th
greatest personality, but they have been overlooke
simply because they aren't as skilled. But can yc
imagine when skill set collides with excellence, not
deed but in heart? That is an unstoppable, favored ar
powerful person.

This is what I mean when I mention, a more excelle
way. It's when all is in alignment as God intended. I
when character, mindset and good works flow from
humble heart. Our daily prayer should be *"teach n*
how to be excellent!" Let's continue to unpack this.

Excellence is to excel and go beyond. Some of you find it difficult to commit to praying daily. Daniel? He prayed three times a day. And he did not pray out of duty, but he prayed because of relationship. He also purposed in his heart that he would not eat the king's meat nor drink his drink. He set his intention first and the power to say no began as a seed in his heart. Set your intention (mind) first and the rest (your attitude, body and behavior) will lead to an excellent spirit.

He could've just decided to be like everyone else and follow the crowd. But he did not want to compromise his relationship with God, so he declined. What have you declined lately because of your purpose? Remember that your purpose is the reason for that which you were created. Once you know your purpose, it serves as a guide. Daniel had a guide as to what to accept and not accept, what to do and what not to do. Are you allowing your purpose to be your guide?

Therefore, Daniel being connected to his God in such a way, through prayer and communication, definitely would've created a solid relationship between the two of them. Through his relationship God showed him his purpose, his reason for being alive and gave him power for service both to God and to man.

Daniel had power alright. He held office in thee kingdoms – Babylon, Media and Persia. Most of us are just trying to propel one business venture, waiting on one idea to take off or to find success in one area. But he was first powerful in spirit that is why he was able to hold and maintain position.

Did you catch that? It's not only about having a catc
mission statement or a great business plan. It's abc
what is happening in your spirit. How's your inside doing
Have you checked inward lately? It wasn't Danie
good looks, nor his works that made him the best choic
or elevated above the rest. It was his spirit. Check yc
spirit.

Your spirit as we have stated previously is the se
where all of your emotions live. Make no mistal
about it. God will promote, prefer and position tho
who will take the time necessary to allow Him
develop their character into one of excellence.

I'm just saying, as much as humanly possible, let your y
be a yes and your no, be your no. That is integral livin
Circumstances arise. We have to live our truth daily. Ar
we do have the power to change our minds. Son
people abuse this, and use it as an advantage to tre
people unfairly. But those who will live and work wi
integrity, will see the fruit of their labor, manifest.

I must highlight here that Daniel (and his friends) we
captured as teenagers from Jerusalem by the Kir
(Nebuchadnezzar). The King gave instructions that h
wanted to capture only the best of the best childre
"those without blemish, good looking, gifted in
wisdom, possessing knowledge and quick to understan
who had the ability to serve in the king's palace, ar
whom they might teach the language and literature..
according to Daniel 1:4.

108

Imagine how it must have been very traumatic to have been captured, especially as child, leaving family, friends, everything familiar behind and not by your choice. That would be a disruption to anyone, much less and especially a child. But God doesn't come to disrupt, He comes only to interrupt your life for a specific purpose and a great lesson to be learned by others as well as yourself.

And so it was evident that even before Daniel was promoted, he had already possessed all the characteristics of not just a leader, but a leader led by the spirit. Did you get that? Daniel was captured because he was already excellent. I cannot stress enough, how important it is that you not carry the bold spirit of envy within you towards anyone. What you see in others that comes naturally, carries with it some form of weight, attention, responsibility that you may not be equipped or have the capacity to handle.

Can I also reiterate that what you are, is already down on the inside of you? What I mean is that you may be overshadowed by the self doubt, low self esteem and a poor image of self. But if you ever stopped to first realize that you are perfectly imperfectly and that with God's help you have the ability to tap into your personal power of who you already are, you would become unstoppable. It's already in you. Say it aloud "It's already in me."

Additionally, it's never too early or too late to b
excellent. If as a teen Daniel had characteristics th
were admirably even to his very enemy, then that leav
you with zero excuses to become excellent in every wo
beginning now. So whether in big amounts or sm
doses make it your intention today to grow in one
more area.

You've heard the saying, *start where you are.* Don't wo
until you are over booked to act like a professional. Ha
a professional mindset even when the space doesn't c
for it. Don't wait until you're in the company of who
who to step up your game. Don't dress for where yo
are; dress for where you're headed. Don't second gue
your seat at the table when it was favor that reserve
your spot. Don't just do your homework but comple
your assignments.

Get systems in place. Become organized. Increase yo
vocabulary. Read books. Listen to podcasts. Wato
videos that enlighten and inspire. Learn something ne
every day. Be adventurous. And don't be afraid
tackle, learn from subject matters or cultures that diff
from yours or from what is your norm. If "no new friends"
your mantra, then just ensure that the ones you alrea
have, keep you growing, not just going.

Treat your only client, only member, only supporter as
they are the most important person in the worl
because they are. Another one of my favorite quotes is
*was raised to treat the janitor with same respect as th
CEO."*

Back to Daniel, our reference. Once captured, he maintained his integrity in the things that made him who he was (his diet, his lifestyle, his worship, his work, his God). That is a word and a formula for somebody right there. Daniel didn't display a foul attitude. He didn't plan or partake in a pity party. And he did not even try to start a riot.

I'm not certain how many of can say there were able to maintain self control during brutal trials. But Daniel was just being true to himself. He was a leader who was excellent before the challenges and he remained one in spite of. That is actually what got him the promotion.

Are you familiar with the Daniel Fast? It is one of the most known ways that believers and non believers practice self restraint in order to create their own spiritual and personal discipline in cleansing their bodies and their hearts. Usually over a period of 21 days, a diet is adapted based on abstaining from meat. Instead more fruits, vegetables and water is incorporated.

Can you imagine being the kind of leader that impacts people globally, even centuries later, long after you're gone? How awesome to be benefiting from a sacred commitment you made prior? Yes, Daniel is still preferred today.

It was his ability to remain in character, no matter how many scene changes he experienced. Many of you are in character, but it is not serving you, your purpose, your work nor your God very well. It might be time to close the

curtain on that tired act and get ready for a ne
performance for an audience of one, God.

I was reading a blog where the writer mentioned th
she was hired for a seasonal position but the season w
coming to an end. She feared she was getting ready
be fired so she immediately began spending time in th
backroom, which made her become very familiar wi
the company's product. In fact, more familiar than th
other employees that stayed in the front space of th
business.

Here's a key point. How many of you are willing to stay
the back, work in silence, work on your business and wc
on yourselves? Trust and believe where you go, you v
know. If you spend due time in the right area, in dt
season you will be promoted.

This writer's confidence grew in herself and the compar
because she knew the products so well that oth
employees began to ask her for answers to their produ
related questions. Many of you are wondering, why is
that others can appear so confident? Or maybe yc
want to increase your own self confidence.

I can't say it enough. Spend more time finding out wh
you are than you do thinking about what everyone el
has to say about you and your life. Your confidence v
grow because you will get to know your product in suc
a way, that for every question, every misconceptic
you'll have an answer. And that product is you. Th
product is your purpose. It's the reason why you we
born and were created. But you have to put in the time

Soon after, this employee took on more responsibilities. She learned new skills that were outside of what was required of her. This is the excellence and the going above and beyond we are speaking of here. This is a more excellent way to do things.

However, let me also stick a pin here and mention that being excellent does come with more responsibilities. Are you ready for that? Excellence is not a destination; it is continuous clean up, ever learning, always growing, never stopping, remaining brilliant, being a light, an example, shining even in the most adverse situations.

So then, with more responsibilities, comes additional work. Did you hear that? Additional WORK. This is one of the reasons that I am baffled that people can become jealous and envious of what is essentially someone's *responsibilities*. It may look like a blessing and it is. It may seem like preference and it probably is. It may have been favor and that could be the case.

But at the end of the day, whatever you see somebody with, or whatever they have, know that although it may be a blessing, preference or favor, it is also most definitely a responsibility! Now the question is, are you ready for that kind of responsibility? And no one really knows how much they can bear until they begin to carry their own load.

Once this employee began to take on the new responsibilities and did an excellent job in each area, her boss began to take notice. Yes, God will begin to notice your efforts to do good, be better and to become excellent. This is really who you really want to please a way. Your utmost desire must be to please God. God your boss. If you keep working, keep it clean, keep it u eventually, He will take notice!

And so one day, her boss called her into his office ar gave her more responsibilities (you will never get awo from responsibilities) and added the phrase she hc probably been longing to hear "You have bee promoted." Somebody is waiting on a promotic Someone is waiting on a deal to go through. Others a waiting on a deposit into their account. There are son individuals that are longing for success in business.

You will receive your promotion by adapting "a mo excellent way." You will be promoted when you ha' grown in a certain area. You will be preferred when yc have gone above and beyond. You will be elevate when you have shown maturity in one area or anoth You will excel when you have exceeded expectatior And...it's in that order.

Now this is not to say that those who are schemers ar undermining won't be fruitful. They will definitely be fruit. And it will look and appear attractive to those wi carnal minds and carnal spirits. But a closer inspectic one day in their presence, once they open up the mouths, you will soon observe that not all fruit is goc fruit. Some fruit is spoiled. And what do you do wi spoiled fruit? Eventually, it gets thrown out.

The seed might've been planted correctly. It w growing nicely. But somewhere along the way, something happened to it. Or maybe, it's past bearing season. Could it be that it was left hanging too long? Perhaps the elements got to it. Elements like **jealousy, intimidation, fear, pride** or **anger**. Don't allow anything to destroy your good seed or spoil your fruit.

Speaking of fruit, if your spirit bears fruit, what kind of fruit should you should be harvesting?

I'm glad you want to know.

The Fruit of the Spirit

I think we've unequivocally established that your spirit can bear "negative" fruit.

Obviously the kind of fruit your spirit produces will be indicative of your character and emotions. Here's the thing, the Creator already knows what He's working with when it comes to your inner being. And it's up to you to make time for a check up on your spiritual health.

I once heard someone who I admire say that there comes a point in your life when God wants to evaluate you. How about you take the initiative to check your own intentions, mindset and feelings? You need to check in daily to ensure that everything is in alignment with His desire for your life in attitude, behavior, disposition and matters of the heart.

Know that you will eventually be consumed by what you are. To ignore foul or spoiled fruit is to welcome detrimental seasons of spiritual death by natural causes. You may ask, *so what am I checking for? How can I ensure that I'm striving for what is healthy or what do I need to do in order to reset my negative emotions?*

I am a person that loves to live by lists. They help me to stay organized. Having a list keeps me on track and I am able to gage my productivity even at a glance. To break it down, there is a biblical term called "the fruit of the spirit" that list and provide nine ways in which you can ensure you are investing in your personal and spiritual development, not your demise. Meditate on the characteristic of each to plant healthy seeds that will bear good fruit now.

According to Galatians 5:22-23 the fruit of the Spirit is:

love
giving or doing freely whether the person deserves it or not and not looking for anything in return

joy
unlike happiness which occurs when something good *happens*, joy is independent of happiness and is possible to demonstrate even during challenging times. One must be focused on the problem solver (God), not the problem (circumstance), in order to fulfill joy

peace
unexplainable content even in the midst of chaos

longsuffering
the ability not to lash out or pay back evil for evil

gentleness
displaying kindness without malice

goodness
exercising genuine care that others do well, even if you have to help sharpen them to brilliance

faith

being a solid example for others by consistently showing up in your God-given gifts, ready to complete your God-given assignments

meekness

not for the headstrong but to be meek is to allow peace to rule, rest and remain in you and through you

temperance

deliberate self control over fleshly and soulish desires and allowing God's Spirit to control your life

These are not *fruits*, as in the plural form. The fruit of the spirit is one fruit with what could be defined as nine attributes. So having high tolerance is not marked "done" for the category of longsuffering and then receiving low check marks for temperance because you have an anger problem. If you're going to reset your emotions, you cannot reset halfway. It's a full reset which will manifest complete transformation of mind, soul and spirit.

Nothing becomes a fruit unless it was first in seed form. Believe it or not, there is some level of a seed for the nine attributes in each and every one of us. Checking in, is ensuring that you cultivate that seed until it becomes the full blown, ripe, ready to be the shared fruit it is supposed to be.

You've heard the term 'a work in progress'? Well, for many, your seed is not only progressive but it is also a

work in process. Keep nourishing your seed. Protect you
seed from outside elements that would have your seed
die. Don't abort your seed by giving into temptation.

There's no sliding into excellence or hoping to be better
To manifest the fruit of the spirit in your life daily, is to
subscribe to intentional living along with you and God co
creating, as He helps you to manifest your purpose (the
reason why you were born), here on earth.

Now to Deactivate, Finally.

Throughout this entire book we have explored five familiar emotions and what are deemed five bold spirits that crumble any progress to living a life of excellence inward and outwardly. You now have a positive blueprint of the more excellent way that you should be striving for and what kind of fruit you should be producing out of your spirit, daily.

If you are ever going to master your emotions in a healthy way, the first order of business is to get out of your feelings. This is the first process to deactivating emotionalism that cause more harm than good. To live or constantly be in your feelings and keep your spirit healthy at the same time is contrary one to the other.

We've already mentioned that feelings are not facts and to depend on your feelings is to be fickle and moody because your feelings will change. Yet, there are those feelings that linger long enough to cause a seed of *jealousy, intimidation, fear, pride* and *anger* to take root. So what do you need to do? How do you deactivate and reset?

Understand that we are indeed emotional beings. That is the way God made us. What's important here is to have the ability to recognize what is going to allow you to become whole and what is designed to poke holes at God's design, which is your life. Additionally, once the negative feelings arise, what you do with them in the

next moments is crucial to spiritual survival and person
success.

To deactivate negative roots, is to be able to separa
what is a feeling and what is a fact. For example, if yo
are struggling to produce good fruit in one area of yo
life, you cannot sit around and wait for a feeling
change to come over you. You must understand th
you cannot live contrary to God's plan for your life n
matter how you feel at any given moment.

To deactivate negative roots, is to evaluate yo
emotions based on the fruit we should be producin
We've already defined the nature of our fruit. Now v
must do due diligence and see if our feelings are
harmony with those attributes. Read again the nir
attributes of the Spirit.

If they are not, we must deactivate our feelings. And
you find it difficult to do so, then give yourself c
emotional deadline. Don't let that negative emotic
continue to ride out and carry you all the way throug
life. Give it a due date of how long you will allow yours
to feel that way. Then get ready for the ultimate reset!

To deactivate negative roots is to take time to ident
the source of your negative emotions. While your feelin
aren't always factual, they do hold slight clues as w
they are there. Ignoring them, avoiding the
suppressing and repressing them will be catastrophic
and of itself.

Are there any past hurt or disappointments that you are holding on to?

Are you sinning against your own self and feeling heavy by the weight of guilt and shame? Your feelings can often shed light on a deeper matter, a matter of the heart, and guide you to a path where the load can be lightened.

To deactivate negative roots is to honestly compare your emotions with God's word. The good news is there is no condemnation only reconciliation. It will be a renewal of your heart being entwined with His will. That really is living with inward bliss here on earth. Because God is in the business of reconciliation.

Once you are crystal clear on what the degree of separation is, you can humbly submit your emotions, your feelings back to the One who created you. Remember He knows your frame. He knows that you are human. He understands how you are wired. He is very much acquainted with what makes you tick. Staying addicted to your negative emotions and flaws in character is a disservice to not only yourself but to your Creator also.

To deactivate negative roots is to not allow yourself to become a victim over and over again. Stop replaying, regurgitating and revisiting what happened. It's time to change the station. Sing a new song. Get up and get going in a new direction.

To deactivate negative roots is to be able to unapologetically declare what you want and what your innate needs are. Most of the time negative feeling arise because your needs are not being met by you standards, value or expectations. Do the inner work t get to the core by listing and writing down what it that you most need so that you can receive guidance on how to attain it.

In essence, to deactivate negative roots is to perforn a daily Spirit Check. Check Your Feelings. If they ar out of sorts and are keeping you off kilter, there nothing wrong with taking a few needful moments t calm yourself, mentally remove yourself of all thoughts, center yourself by being mindful and in th moment and focusing on God, what you need, hov you want to feel and then finally, exhale to experienc a mental shift, physical and emotional shift as well.

Your spirit is hungry for what is healthy. Become you soul's nutritionist and live whole ever after, **masterfully**.

Acknowledgments

My partner in life and husband, **Restee Collins, III**...you allow me the space to create, the time to grow, the room to expand and the encouragement to keep moving forward. You are my solid rock.

Destiny, Charisma and Restee, IV...I am forever grateful that God chose me to be your mom. My desire is that you exceed the expectations of your Dad and I, to become your best self in the highest form possible. Without even knowing, your existence rescues me many times over. I aim to make you proud.

My parents, **Neville and Hope Harris**...You raised me to let spirituality be my life's guide and laid a solid foundation on which even today, I still stand firmly on. Thank you.

To all the many friends, mentors, spiritual examples and individuals near and far, living and deceased who have impacted my life in a remarkable way, knowingly and unknowingly, inspiring me to keep going and growing...I thank you.

Thank you to the online community of friends, entrepreneurs, supporters, moms and daughters of The Persona Program...for allowing me to be an inspiration, that ultimately motivates towards transformation. Because you have shared your life, your gifts and given me support, it has mandated this growth that I have experienced. I'm grateful for your presence in my life.

To my Lord and Savior, Jesus Christ...You know who I am and you still chose and called me for such a time as this. Thank you for revealing me to myself and simultaneously revealing yourself to me. I have matured to trust your master plan. Our relationship is like the air I breathe, necessary.

About the Author

Michelle Collins is a dynamic Speaker. As a Coach, her quest is for entrepreneurs of faith, believers and leaders to stay connected spiritually, while they are building their brands, ministries and their lives. She uses each platform to share spiritual insights for practical living. Through individual or group mentorship, she encourages redeeming work and creative aspirations to flow.

Michelle is a Los Angeles Sparks Ambassador and the L.A. Sparks 2015 #WeAreWomen honoree, highlighting the accomplishments, leadership and empowerment of women in their community. She has also received commendation from the County of Los Angeles in recognition for her dedicated service in her community. Her written work has been featured on Maria Shriver's Architects of Change, a title given to those committed to move humanity forward.

A mother of three, she motivates moms raising daughter to Be Whole + Parent Well. Her WORKbook (also available in eBook format), a journal style stimulus, "30 Ways in 30 Days to Be That Mom" encourages moms to thrive and essentially strive to #BeThatMom. These sound parenting practices provide nourishment of the soul for both mother and daughter.

In 2007, she founded The Persona Program and as Program Director, she prepares a generation of girls 7 – 18 years old for positive presentation through a mission to build Confidence, develop Character and promote proper Conduct. The organization also serves as t(w)eenspiration and validation that unlocks the dreams of the inner little girl.

A FIDM alum, with a degree in Fashion Merchandising and Marketing, a former Image Consultant and having vast experience in both the fashion and beauty industries as an Event Producer, Education Manager and College Representative all set the groundwork to implement powerful programs, develop curriculum and host celebrated events for girls and women. Each gathering provides tools and resources needed to personify their innate beauty and tap into their God-given potential.

A wife of 17 years, she resides in Southern California with her family.

www.michelleharriscollins.com | www.thepersonaprogram.org
Facebook + **Instagram** @michelleharriscollins | @personaprogram
Twitter @MHCollins_

For more info, booking or collaborations for speaking engagements, events, workshops or coaching **:CONTACT:** michellenecollins@gmail.com

Made in the USA
San Bernardino, CA
13 November 2017